WIN
in
BUSINESS

**20 keys
to catapult
you towards
your vision**

Peter Irvine
Co-Founder, Gloria Jean's Coffees

Ark House Press
PO Box 163
North Sydney, NSW, 2059
Telephone: (02) 8437 3541; Facsimile (02) 9999 2053
International: +612 8437 3541; Facsimile +612 9999 2053
www.arkhousepress.com

Unless otherwise noted, Scripture quotations are from the Holy Bible, New
International Version, Copyright 1973, 1978, 1984, 1998 by International Bible
Society

Cataloguing in Publication Data:

Irvine, Peter.
Win in business : 20 keys to catapulting your business.

Bibliography.
Includes index.
ISBN 9780980345834 (pbk.).

1. Success in business. 2. Business. I. Title.

650.1

Printed and bound in Australia
Cover design by bbdagency.com

ark house

Endorsements

"I had the pleasure of working closely with Peter for many years in the late 1970s when he was intimately involved with the McDonald's business as a senior executive at DDB Needham, the advertising agency servicing McDonald's where I was a senior executive in the initial years of my own career. In those days, the challenge of establishing the McDonald's brand essence was still a very big one and Peter was a key part of the team that worked so effectively to achieve the initial base of success that is so clearly reflected in the McDonald's brand today in Australia, some 30 years later.

Peter always stood out as a real team player — never overly assertive, but his methods resulted in very effective progress in his own quiet, but steely determined manner. The things that stood out to me in those days were his very high work ethic, combining working very hard with the ability to effectively communicate to all and sundry. He revealed a true sense of care and concern for people in all that he did and this resulted in a deep respect for his views and input to the direction of the McDonald's business in those early days in Australia.

He later went on to put all that experience to good work as one of the key executive team that very successfully developed the Gloria Jean's Coffees organisation in Australia. For me, it was a pleasure to see him leading from the front in that role and putting the experiences of our time together to such effective use in developing his own career path in the Gloria Jean's Coffees world. Obviously, he did that very successfully.

Peter is a true example of the 'quiet achiever', who has been able to let his results do the talking , while at the same time delivering a genuine concern and respect for all those who he had to deal with. I am sure this has been a core basis for his success in business."
Bob Mansfield,
former CEO and Chairman of McDonald's Australia.

"It was my privilege to get to know Peter over 13 years ago and since then we have had occasions to work closely together. One particular time was when I chaired the board of Quest Australia and he was an active and integral fellow board member. I soon appreciated the wealth of his

very hands-on experience that he brought to the table. Peter's input was obviously based on years of working at the 'coal face' of business where he was able to distinguish between what really works against what is more theoretical, which frequently looks good in text books but lacks real impact and effectiveness.

I know Peter will offer tremendous input and ideas in his book that will assist the reader in achieving effective plans for their own organisations and companies, be it in the profit or not-for-profit sectors."
Peter F. S. King,
Immediate past Chairman of World Vision Australia, past Chief Executive Officer of John Fairfax Group, Ex Chairman of Opportunity International, and Board Member of World Vision International.

"Two things I know about Peter Irvine as a result of my 25 years of contact with him in the meeting rooms of DDB Needham Advertising and on the squash court – he's a fierce competitor, which he hides behind a placid easy-going exterior; and he's a very thoughtful individual who makes his own way regardless of popularist or trendy chatter.

Knowing those two things about Peter will make his book compelling reading for me."
Peter Ritchie,
Founding Director of McDonald's Australia.

"When it comes to meeting people who think big, I can't think of anyone else like Peter Irvine. To have a vision for 25 Gloria Jean's Coffees stores and then have the determination and vision to see it grow to over 400, plus take it around the world, that shows the depth of his belief and commitment to following a BIG vision. I'm always inspired whenever I hear him speak, and have learnt many valuable lessons over the years."
Jason Berry,
General Manager, radio station 96five FM, Brisbane, Australia.

"The message I received from Peter Irvine when I first met him was: Never live in other people's mindsets. I considered that advice and reflected upon my own career and those around me and made some changes. To my great surprise, I have learnt that Peter was right. Too often we can be influenced by others and not have the resolve to achieve what we

want or need. Living in the mindsets of others who perhaps are negative or sowing bad seeds into your mind and affecting your confidence can have a direct impact upon what you do and what you achieve. Peter has shown throughout his distinguished career that having a clear focus and an attitude of positive persistence can lead to remarkable things for you and those around you. Mix these competencies with ethical behaviour and a willingness to help others and you begin to understand some of Peter Irvine's core principles… and then understand why he has been so successful.

Someone once said, 'Always listen to a wise man.' Peter Irvine is such a man!"
Richard Evans,
CEO, Franchise Council of Australia

"Peter Irvine met with me regularly during my time working for another company and then starting my own business. He was able to encourage me and provide ideas on how to work with a difficult boss and still be able to exceed targets and build a sales team around the country. I was encouraged to go for it, and eventually the decision was made to resign and start my own business. The advice regarding setting up a warehouse and just the 'nuggets of gold' of business information, direction, encouragement and challenge has catapulted my business significantly forward."
Trent Fitzgibbins,
Director, Jetblack Products Pty Ltd

"In my life I have been fortunate to have been involved with many people who claim to be 'successful'. Peter's success in business and life is a glowing example of what true success is about. Humility, transparency and a genuine love for people are the hallmarks of Peter's life. Peter is not only successful, he is significant, leaving a legacy of how he has helped so many people around the world. This book is another example of Peter's contribution to all of us. Thanks, Peter, for being part of my life."
Tony Gattari,
Managing Director, Achievers Group Pty Ltd

"I actively sought out Peter Irvine in the hope he could provide me with any advice to help me start my business and steer it in the right

direction for the future. I was overwhelmed and eternally grateful. Not only was Peter generous in giving up his time, he also showed a sincere interest and offered sound advice. He has been and still is an inspiration to me and my business, Flowers by Fruit."

Tania Haroulis,
Flowers By Fruit

"Peter has been a close friend and confidante for a period of 30 years… from the early days at DDB Needham Advertising, through the roll-out of Gloria Jean's Coffees in Australia, to the present day. His creative thinking, 'just-do-it' attitude, and the ability to communicate at all levels have stood by him handsomely, and his success is totally deserved. Yet through it all, he remains unassuming and unpretentious.

He is one of the most generous and compassionate men I have known. 'Giving' to others in terms of time, effort, resource and personal advice is one of his special gifts, and his willingness to share his expertise finds special expression in this book. I can recommend this book without reservation."

Dr Ernest F Crocker
BSc (Med) MBBS FRACP DDU, Consultant Physician In Nuclear Medicine

Contents

Introduction...9

Chapter 1   Vision..17

Chapter 2   Manage Your Success.............................29

Chapter 3   Are You in a Comfort Zone?...................35

Chapter 4   Challenges...41

Chapter 5   Stay on Course..49

Chapter 6   People...61

Chapter 7   Be You...75

Chapter 8   Marketing...85

Chapter 9   Keep Learning...97

Chapter 10   Finishing Strong...................................105

Chapter 11   Stop and Change When Necessary....115

Chapter 12   In Travelling Through Life, Travel Light.........121

Chapter 13   Mindsets...129

Chapter 14   Negativity..139

Chapter 15   Honesty and Integrity..........................149

Chapter 16   Family...155

Chapter 17   Partnerships..165

Chapter 18   Get a Coach..175

Chapter 19   Support Your Community....................183

Chapter 20   Franchising..191

To Be Continued...205

Support for Great Community Causes.............209

Acknowledgements..213

Recommended Books...217

About the Author...219

Contact Details & Peter Irvine's Services........221

Introduction

I have had the privilege of working closely with two very successful brands, certainly in Australia: McDonald's and Gloria Jean's Coffees. There have been other businesses and brands I have been involved with along the way, but these are the most well-known. Both have seen remarkable success.

I was part of the team at DDB Needham Advertising that launched McDonald's in Australia in the 1970s. Today there are 730 McDonald's restaurants in Australia. In the 1990s our advertising agency developed the 'MacTime' concept which has become synonymous with any meal time, whether breakfast, morning tea, lunch or supper.

The other brand—Gloria Jean's Coffees—has been lauded as Australia's fastest growing franchise. It has won the Franchise Council of Australia's 2005 'Franchisor of the Year' award, 2006 'National Retailer of the Year' award, 2006 American Express 'Franchise of the Year' award, and 2006 'Emerging Exporter of the Year' award. We started the business in Australia in 1996 with plans to introduce 25 stores in ten years. Today we have well over 400 stores in Australia. In 2006 alone our stores in Australia served around 50 million cups of coffee.

In 2005 we purchased the international brand name for all countries, as well as supply rights for all countries (except the USA and Puerto Rico). This meant inheriting 15 countries. We now have over 750 stores across 30 countries. These include Indonesia, Ireland, Japan, Jordan, Kazakhstan, Kuwait, Malaysia, Mexico, New Zealand, Philippines, Romania, Saudi Arabia, Singapore, South Africa, South Korea, Thailand, Turkey, the United Arab Emirates, the United Kingdom, Vietnam and others.

My Story

I started work in February 1963 at age 14 years and ten months. I had left school with an 'Intermediate Certificate,' which is comparable to Year 9 in Australian schools today. Back then very few young people had parents who could afford to educate their children through Years 10 and 11 of high school, let alone through university. The job opportunities weren't as broad as they are today and so you needed to secure a junior position in a nominated industry.

I found myself in a job with a small advertising agency in Sydney that mainly handled print, newspaper and magazine work. At that time, television was still in its infancy for most advertising agencies. When I started I was grateful for the job. I worked extremely hard for little money, but my job was my future. I was a little young and naïve; it probably took me nine months to realise the company I was working for was an advertising agency. Up until that time I had thought that when you wanted a television commercial the television station would produce it, and that newspapers designed all their own advertisements. I soon realized how wrong I was!

Over the years I progressed through the ranks from dispatch to print production and onto media planning and buying. I eventually became National Media Manager (in charge of media for the agency) and then General Manager of DDB Needham Advertising in Sydney. During that time I spent many years working specifically on the McDonald's account. However, I enjoyed working with a large variety of clients over the years, such as S.C Johnson (a family company that that has been creating innovative cleaning products such as Windex, Ziploc, Pledge, Glade and Edge for over 100 years), The Wrigley Company (the company that produces some of the world's best-known chewing gum brands) and Hasbro (the company that manufactures toys, games, puzzles and much more). My last two years in advertising was as Managing Director of the agency. With a team of dedicated people we were able to build a phenomenal agency—successful, profitable and generating advertising that worked for our clients.

The Gloria Jean's Coffees Story

So what is Gloria Jean's Coffees? It is a specialist coffee concept for people on the go. We serve high quality hot and cold coffee drinks, beans and related merchandise in a friendly, convenient atmosphere. By using takeaway cups, self-serve condiments together with light, pre-prepared food items, we are able to serve our customers quickly. They can take advantage of casual seating areas or simply take their drinks away. The store decor is warm, modern, open and inviting, with stores mostly located in key access positions. The vast majority of our stores in Australia are individually franchised, providing a link through the franchisee with the local community.

I was introduced to Gloria Jean's Coffees in 1995. Sixteen years earlier, Gloria Jean's Coffees began as a single store near Chicago, Illinois (USA). In 1979 the Kvetko family was visiting a small gift shop that sold coffee beans and decided to buy the business. The lady's name was Gloria Jean Kvetko. Due to the increasing popularity of specialty coffees in the mid-1980s, Gloria Jean's Coffees began franchising stores in Chicago. That was the genesis of a global coffee brand.

My friend and later business partner, Nabi Saleh, came to me in 1995 with an idea. Nabi was a successful businessman who today has over 30 years experience in the tea and coffee industry. His passion for coffee began on the coffee plantations of Papua New Guinea where he worked for Australia New Guinea Holdings. In 1978 Nabi took over a medium-sized coffee company called ASCO, increasing its turnover from AUD$250,000 (over USD$213,000) to AUD$15 million (almost USD$13 million). He then went on to establish various coffee and tea family-owned companies.

It was in mid-1995 when Nabi and Angela Saleh approached Sue and me about the opportunity to bring the US-based Gloria Jean's Coffees franchise to Australia. So Nabi and I flew to the US to meet with the owners of Gloria Jean's Coffees. At that time the brand was owned by Brothers Coffees, a retail company producing mainly roasted coffee beans for supermarkets. They understood supermarket products, but not necessarily the franchising and retail business. The company had purchased the brand from Gloria Jean Kvetko herself and was certainly having some success at that time with sites located exclusively in shopping malls.

Although their knowledge was limited in this business, the owners of Brothers Coffees were looking to expand internationally. After we viewed many of their stores and held discussions over a number of days, we decided to purchase the right to open 25 stores in Australia within the first ten years. For us at that time, 25 stores was a huge vision. Little did we know that in that ten-year timeframe (to November 2006) we would have well over 400 stores in Australia. Nor did we imagine that at that time we would also purchase the franchise rights for the brand worldwide, including the rights to supply product to every country except the USA and Puerto Rico. With the international purchase we inherited 15 countries, many of whom were not successful through lack of training and operational support.

In 2005 we purchased the brand worldwide to reposition Gloria Jean's Coffees globally based on the widely successful Australian model. Despite the many subsequent obstacles, we began to put into position the different elements needed to become a second major player in the world. These included trademark registrations, branding, signage, store design, standard drink menu boards, standard recipes and ingredient supply.

Today Gloria Jean's Coffees is known as a specialty coffee concept for people on the go. We have premium coffee sourced directly from plantations (so the growers get the price that's negotiated for them), roasted to specifications, and prepared in-store by well-trained staff. Our coffee beans are not sourced through the general coffee market, but directly from plantations in coffee growing countries around the world. Prices are negotiated in order to maintain a sustainable lifestyle for the growers and to ensure ongoing quality crops (for instance, trees are husbanded correctly). We also purchase Rainforest Alliance coffees wherever possible. These coffees are grown on farms which are certified by 'Rainforest Alliance' (a non-profit conservation organization) as being managed according to the highest environmental and social standards. This includes protecting the welfare of coffee farmers and their families, wildlife and their habitat, the conservation of waterways, soils and trees.

They warned us we would fail

When Gloria Jean's Coffees started in Australia in 1996, experts in the coffee and franchising industries warned us that we would fail. They advised us that Australians would not embrace flavoured coffee or take-away coffee cups. To succeed, Gloria Jean's Coffees would have to break through a number of mindsets. Today we have succeeded beyond even our own expectations. And we have changed the Australian coffee drinking culture and set trends in the coffee industry. For instance, we introduced frequent sippers cards to the industry. We also introduced chai tea latte as a drink to the mass market in Australia in 2000; these days you will find chai tea latte in almost every café and restaurant.

When we started in Australia, people told us to change the name because it sounded more like a fashion store than a coffee retailer. I guess they thought we sold jeans. We had to remind those people that we only had the name under license, so we didn't have the ability to change it. In franchising, you can't just change the name. In any case, I have found that you can build a brand around the name. When McDonald's launched in Australia, no one automatically associated the name with hamburgers. When Dominos launched, no one knew it as a pizza franchise.

It's not the name itself that will determine your success, it's how you build the brand. Today over 85 percent of Australians recognise the Gloria Jean's Coffees name and recognise that it relates to specialty coffee. That is a fantastic testament to the brand's success. Many other companies who spend a great deal more than we do on advertising and have been in the market for considerably longer have only managed to achieve a much smaller percentage of recognition.

People have asked me, "Why leave advertising and move into a totally different industry?" Well, I gained franchising experience when I ran the McDonald's account. And I learned a lot about retail when I managed the advertising accounts of many other companies in industries such as hardware and fashion. Along with my marketing and advertising experience, this all gave me an enormous amount of experience to bring to Gloria Jean's

Coffees. However, I must admit that even with all this prior experience, the learning curve was a steep one!

The main reason for the change in industry — the 'higher cause' if you like — was a passion both Sue and I had to own and operate a business which could generate funds for worthwhile causes. We were excited about an opportunity to bless people with rewarding careers and a business concept that would continue to do so beyond our own working lives. In our partners, Nabi and Angela Saleh, we found people whose dream dovetailed our own.

Learn from the past, but move forward

This varied and rich experience gives me the opportunity to share with you the many business and life gems I have collected along my journey. In this book I will share with you some of the stories from my advertising days with DDB Needham Advertising, as well as from my time at Gloria Jean's Coffees. My intention in writing this book is for you to learn, to be encouraged, and to be challenged that there are opportunities in front of you, not behind you. I want to urge you to stop living in the past; to stop pitching your tent at past successes or failures. Certainly learn from past experiences, but you have to put these behind you in order to move forward.

The lessons I will share with you in this book have the potential to readjust mindsets that may be holding you back from reaching your goals and dreams. I am a practical man, and the lessons I will share with you in this book are practical. If you apply them to your business, career, relationships and other endeavours, they will change your life — as they have vastly enriched mine.

I am convinced that we are here on this earth to succeed. I don't believe we're here to simply get by and pay the bills. Our lot in life is not just to go to work and wait for retirement. If it is all about us, then I believe our lives will eventually become empty and we will quickly become dissatisfied with life. But when we realise a purpose beyond ourselves — that we are able to assist those with greater needs and help people enter into a better quality of life — then our existence takes on a whole new meaning!

As a company, Gloria Jean's Coffees has set out to become successful so that we can contribute to the effectiveness of other people and organisations, like schools, charities and churches. In 2005 we entered into a partnership with an organisation called Compassion to support 300 children in a village in Brazil. In 2004 the New South Wales Government (in Australia) approached us to open a store in a women's correctional centre, and we agreed. These women have been robbed of hope. So we have opened a Gloria Jean's Coffees store in that correctional centre and employ these women to run it, giving them valuable training for their future. Their children regularly visit them and the relaxed store atmosphere—together with a playground installed by the centre—provides a safe, unthreatening environment.

However, our ongoing key focus is a charity called Mercy Ministries, a residential program for young women in crisis. Currently there are two Mercy Ministries homes in Australia—one in Queensland and one in New South Wales—and further homes are opening around the country from 2007. Through our involvement internationally, Mercy Ministries has already opened a home in the United Kingdom and further homes are tabled to open in other countries around the world. We are committed to continually raising funds to support this charity. Our stores are able to help donate funds and increase awareness of Mercy Ministries by placing cash donation boxes and promotional leaflets on their counters. In October every year in Australia we run the 'Cappuccino for a Cause' weekend during which 50 cents from every one of our Cappuccinos or Cappuccino Chillers is donated to Mercy Ministries. We plan to expand our involvement with Mercy Ministries internationally wherever we open in a new country.

Life is a journey, not a destination

Every person, business and venture needs a purpose. And to achieve that purpose, we must recognize that life is a journey, not a destination. We haven't arrived when we get married. We haven't arrived when we start a business. And we certainly haven't arrived when we are born on this earth. These are just dots along our journey. Like any journey, we will face all kinds of obstacles and difficulties, and we will also experience periods of excitement and joy. Whilst we will never arrive at a destination in any part of life here on earth, we should always strive to keep learning, growing and improving.

At some point along the way, the challenges of life can dull our excitement and our commitment so that many of us lose a sense of passion for life. At that point, many of us check out of life. Whether in our relationships, in our sporting endeavours or in our business, our passions and desires often desert us. This should not happen. In this book I want to show you how to recapture your passion so that you can rejoin the journey of a fulfilling life, one that God has planned and purposed for you.

I trust that when you read this book you will be challenged to grow to new levels in your business, your relationships and in other areas of your life. After all, as we say at Gloria Jean's Coffees, life's too short to drink bad coffee!

Peter Irvine

one |

VISION

"The greatest danger for most of us is not that our aim is too high and we miss it, but that it is too low and we achieve it." – Michelangelo

"Where there is no vision, people perish…" - Proverbs 29:18

The great American author and activist Helen Keller contracted an illness at 19 months of age that eventually left her both deaf and blind. Later in life she stated, "The only thing worse than being blind is having sight but no vision." What's your vision like? Where do you see yourself in five, ten or 20 years?

Before we started Gloria Jean's Coffees, we wrote down our vision, mission and values for our company. We did that so our staff and our customers could see where we were heading and what we stood for. Our vision was: "To be the most respected and loved coffee company in Australia." It was a fairly bold and broad statement, especially back then, but it kept all of us focused on the journey.

As we set out on our maiden voyage in those early years, we felt that aiming at any number of stores in the first ten years — whether 10, 50 or 100 — would have been a big, bold vision. Today, just over ten years since we began, having opened over 450 stores in Australia alone, we know we have reached a significant level of achievement, way beyond our initial expectations.

In fact, in February 2005 we purchased the Gloria Jean's Coffees brand worldwide from the US owners. At the same time, we also took over the supply of products to our stores worldwide. We inherited 14 Master Franchises in 15 countries around the world. So our vision then became: "To be the most respected and loved coffee company in the world."

That is still a big, bold statement, but Gloria Jean's Coffees is on a path to making that vision a reality. That vision influences the people we hire, the strategic plans we put in place, the funding that is required, and the actions required to achieve that vision. Back then, no one knew us as a brand, so we had to set about building our brand. Over the ensuing years we established national brand awareness not only through our retail outlets — our stores across Australia — but also through our marketing and public relations efforts.

Don't be scared of big visions

Poet and avant-garde film artist James Broughton once said, "The only limits are, as always, those of vision." I want to encourage you to grab a hold of a strong, bold, large vision for your business. Even if you don't achieve that vision in your lifetime, you are going to have a lot of fun and excitement attempting to reach a vision of that magnitude. You set the vision and the plans, and then watch it grow and exceed your expectations. So don't be scared of big visions. Start to visualize an exciting vision for your business right now. Capture it in your heart and in your mind.

In 2005 I was speaking to a business group and at the end of my talk a business associate came to me and said, "My vision has been very small." Up until that point, his business had one branch and he was very comfortable just getting by at the current level. But I had challenged this businessman that there was more to life; that his business was going to lose its market position if he didn't expand his vision. He came to the realization that he needed to do something about the business, so he decided to expand his vision, and he made the decision to open a second branch. However, he didn't put in place plans on how he was going to do that. As a result, he neglected to properly invest in both branches.

This business associate saw me recently and said that he is finally looking to set his vision in motion by putting in place the focus and the plans to build the two businesses. He again admitted that his original vision had been a small one. In fact, even doubling the size with a second branch, the expansion still reflected fairly small thinking. He is now wrestling with the idea of opening even more branches and then franchising the business.

A close friend of mine recently left his employer to open his own business with some partners. His vision was very expansive. He had very big thinking. I notice that as he grows, not only does his vision remain bold, but he is also progressively working out that vision and expanding to greater levels. He is constantly working on many areas of his business, including the back room office, technology, warehousing, shipping, supply, and the brand name. He is constantly asking for advice, reviewing what he is doing, and putting those plans in place. Just like my friend, you need to have a bold vision, but in the end you need to put the plans in place or you will never achieve your vision.

There are many advantages to having a large vision. One great benefit to owning a bold vision is that it will allow others to sow into what you are doing. When people identify with your vision, mission, values and action plan, they will want to get on board. If you believe in it, and people see that you believe in it, they will back you and come and work for you. And in many cases, people will be willing to help finance your vision. Why? Because it is large, imaginative and captivating!

Author and speaker Steve Penny once said, "Vision releases resources." He explained that we don't attract resources or support for our vision by talking about needs or problems. He said that instead we attract support by communicating vision, because vision attracts people to us.

Passion fuels vision

Author Dr Ken Hemphill stated, "Passion fuels vision and vision is the focus of passion. Leaders who are passionate will create vision and fulfill it." How passionate are you about your vision? If you aren't excited about your vision, how can you expect others to capture and follow the vision? Get passionate about your business and the vision will expand and draw others into it.

Author and leadership expert John Maxwell talked about the law of 'buy-in'. He said that people buy into a leader before they accept that leader's vision. Once they believe the leader, they generally follow his or her vision. The lesson here is that the leader's credibility precedes the leader's plan. If you're not a credible leader, if people aren't buying into your vision, then perhaps you need to focus on your own development first.

In my last two years as managing director at DDB Needham Advertising, we set about building the vision for the agency. Every staff member had been involved in the planning process by the time we presented the completed vision. As a result, the staff all came on the journey for an incredibly successful two years.

Some years ago, in line with our core values, we decided that Gloria Jean's Coffees would support Mercy Ministries—a residential program for young women in crisis—as our core charity. At that time we presented to our franchise family the vision that we had to support Mercy Ministries. We had graduates from the Mercy Ministries program share with our franchise family about how their lives had been changed for the better. We invited the founder of Mercy Ministries in the USA to come and outline the organization's needs. She told us personal stories of young women whose lives had been turned around.

The vision for this alliance came across with such passion that everyone at that presentation wholeheartedly supported the Mercy Ministries program. They embraced the Mercy Ministries coin collection boxes which were placed on store counters and they invested—sowed—into what became the annual Mercy Ministries fundraiser weekend. They saw the vision and, without question, wanted to be a part of it. Great vision presented with passion does that to people!

When we held our regional franchise meetings three times a year, one of the things we were able to do successfully was to theme these meetings around the values of the company. At these meetings we set out our vision, mission and values. Each of the meetings was themed around one of our corporate values. So over a period of 12 to 18 months, each franchisee was reminded of the values of the company — not just in words, but in a practical sense through training and through the marketing programs.

Without a strong vision, you and your staff have nothing to look forward to. A weak vision doesn't instill hope in the future — for you, your staff and your customers. When there is no hope in the future, we lack power in the present. An expansive, imaginative vision is so important to instilling hope in the future. When you and your staff have great hope for the future of your business, there is added motivation. When there is hope in the air, there is an extra bounce in every step. Staff members are glad to turn up at work, and your customers notice the difference.

Most of us aim too low

It is a sad fact that for most of us, we aim too low. Whether it's our business or our career, so often we believe that we need to have a vision that is small and easily achievable. We determine in our minds that we simply need to be realistic, because we don't want to set ourselves up for disappointment. The truth is that our small thinking — our small vision — is limiting what we really could be achieving. When we aim low, there's no growth, and our lives begin to stagnate.

I want to tell you that if you shoot at nothing, you will hit it every time. Aim for something big and bold, and you're likely to hit something of worth. People who think big have expansive thinking. When you don't set limits, you catapult yourself along the journey. In contrast, a small, achievable vision hinders your progress; you end up only managing progress within your comfort zone and according to what you can control.

Obviously, any vision takes time to achieve, especially the bold, exciting ones. No vision evolves into results overnight, but the great thing about vision is that it gives you long-term perspective.

It sets you on a journey over a period of time. Some people think they've arrived and succeeded the day they start their business or the day they get married or the moment they start any new endeavour in life. These people neglect to realize that it's just the start, that it's a process.

When we begin a new venture, having a vision reminds us that the journey has just begun. In fact, it tells us that we are on a course towards a destination. It may be a long and winding road and there will be obstacles and challenges along the route, but a vision will keep us on track, because it reminds us that we are on a journey towards a destination. Author Joseph Murphy once said, "We go where our vision is."

Without a strong vision, hindrances will come along and drag us off course. You may have heard of this ancient proverb: "If you chase two rabbits, both will escape." So pay attention to one goal at a time. One of the most important principles in both our life and our business is that we must be focused on what we are doing so that we actually catch the right rabbit. In business, unless you have a strong focus on your vision, distractions that look like wonderful opportunities will tempt you away from what you are meant to be doing. You will spend your time on those distracting activities and yet they will not produce the right results for you.

Problems can drag you off course

Problems can also drag you off course. We all face problems, but the difference between success and failure is how we respond to problems. If a problem comes along, don't lose your focus or you will move away from your original goal.

When we started Gloria Jean's Coffees in Australia in 1996, a friend came to me and said that we needed to forget about opening retail stores. He said that instead we should be selling everything off a website. "The Internet is the way of the future," he told me. Well, it certainly has been for many businesses. But if we had followed his advice, we would be out of business today. You see, in those days people were buying very little off websites. In fact, the business my friend was in moved across to a web-based strategy and it has struggled to become established ever since. I believe Gloria Jean's Coffees would not be where it is today if we had compromised our vision. Gloria Jean's Coffees would not be the success it is today if we had begun to focus on simply selling coffee from our website.

So set your direction in concrete. At the same time, continually evaluate the things you are doing against your original vision. Many new ideas and ventures may seem profitable at first, but they may also draw you away from your vision. Some may even seem logical extensions to your core vision. But beware! They may become so time-consuming that they move you away from your vision and you end up not producing the results you wanted.

In the early days at Gloria Jean's Coffees, we were asked many times to invest in coffee carts — mobile coffee units with espresso facilities for hire at events. Eventually we had carts designed and we began utilizing them as we worked out the operating bugs. We later realized that they were not part of our core vision. The lesson was learned after problems arose. Not only did these carts prove difficult to move around, they were also hard work to maintain and operate. They needed high voltage power outlets, rarely available at sporting venues or parks. They also needed a source of clean water, a mobile fridge to store vast quantities of milk, some protection against the elements for the staff, a four-wheel-drive vehicle to tow them, level ground, clear access for setting up, and strong muscles! During that early stage, the mobile cart program proved a distraction from our core vision, which was supported by our mission statement: "Gloria Jean's Coffees is committed to building a unified family, consistently serving the highest quality coffee and providing outstanding personalized service in a vibrant store atmosphere."

Walt Disney had a powerful vision. Among his many achievements, the one that he was most excited about in his later years was EPCOT Center (an Experimental Prototype Community of Tomorrow). Disney died in 1966, before it was complete. When EPCOT Center opened in 1982, someone said, "Isn't it a shame he never lived to see his idea realized?"

One of Disney's creative people answered: "But he did see it—that's why it's here!"

Now that's vision! And that's staying the course! His vision was so real that he didn't need to wait and see the real thing. In his mind he already saw the vision completed.

It is my personal belief that the best visions and innovative ideas come from God. Steve Penny once said, "Vision is a God thing. What puts fire in your bones? It is not what you see with your eyes or what you hear with your ears. It is that fire inside you."

Inspiring examples of vision

Vision and imagination are intertwined. Albert Einstein said, "Imagination is more important than knowledge." And actor Donald Curtis stated, "We are what and where we are, because we have first imagined it." Author Henry J. Taylor once stated, "Imagination lit every lamp... built every church, made every discovery, performed every act of kindness and progress, created more and better things for more people. It is the priceless ingredient for a better day." So many men and women throughout history would attest to this. Here are some inspiring examples of people with great vision who achieved so much:

Anesthesia: How would you like to be operated on without anesthetic? That was the way they did it until a Scottish doctor named James Simpson introduced us to artificial sleep. One day he read Genesis 2:21: "The Lord God caused a deep sleep to fall on Adam..." Simpson thought that chloroform might be the answer, so he experimented on himself. In 1847 the first three operations took place. One of the patients was a young soldier who enjoyed it so much that he seized the sponge and inhaled it again. Simpson encountered opposition, but he went on to prove that this was how God operated on Adam.

Braille: In 1824 Louis Braille invented a system of raised dots on paper that blind people could read. He invented 63 symbols representing every language.

Morse code: You and I owe our mobile phone and our computer to a man named Samuel Morse, the inventor of Morse code. One day a friend said to him, "Morse, when you were experimenting, did you ever come to an absolute deadlock, not knowing what to do?"

Morse replied, "More than once!"

"What did you do then?" his friend asked.

Morse shared his secret: "I got down on my knees and prayed for light, and light came..."

Pasteurization: Louis Pasteur, the great French scientist, showed us that infection is a result of something we can't see, namely germs. He eventually introduced methods that saved the lives of millions.

The vacuum cleaner: HC Booth invented the vacuum machine in the American Midwest. As he was sitting in a rocking chair on his porch watching the wind blowing up the dust, he thought to himself: "What if we could get air to suck in the dust?" Later that year, the vacuum cleaner was invented.

Great vision will always attract criticism. Achievers throughout history all faced 'negative input' from people around them. If you have a bold vision and you haven't yet experienced opposition, you can be sure that you will, sooner or later. Statements like "That can't be achieved!" or "You'll never do that!" often precede great success!

When we set out to buy the Gloria Jean's Coffees brand worldwide, we were told that it would never work, that we couldn't run it from Australia, that the contrasting cultures would be a problem, and that exporting product from Australia would be too much of a challenge. "You will not be able to have a standard drinks menu around the world," they said. You know, these people were probably right, but we went out and did it anyway, because we had a vision.

Find a vision that's right for you

So how do you create a vision? What's the process of discovering and defining a vision that is right for you or for your business? Well, a vision often starts with something that is birthed deep within us. American writer, actor, economist and lawyer Ben Stein has said, "The indisputable first step to getting the things you want in life is this: Decide what you want." Your vision already exists in your heart and in your mind. It's been there all along. You simply haven't done much with it.

Ask yourself this question: What is my passion? What is it that excites me? You see, what you are passionate about will most likely be the core of your vision. If you are passionate about providing people with beautiful haircuts, then develop a vision around that. If you are passionate about teaching people about healthy exercise, then that is the core of your vision. Find your passion, and a powerful vision will follow.

Activate your vision

But what do you do with that vision once you have it? Well, the Book of Habakkuk in the Old Testament gives us three instructions on what to do:

1)   **Get the vision clear**
2)   **Write it down and make it succinct**
3)   **Say it out loud** (Habakkuk 2:2).

If you can't see the vision clearly in your own mind, then you can't write it down in a few words. And if you can't say it out loud, you are not committed to it. And if you aren't committed to it, no one else will be!

Writing down your vision helps you communicate your vision to the people around you. It enables you to carry a copy in your wallet or purse. It enables you to stick it up on your bathroom mirror where you can see it every morning and night. You may want to place it on your desk or learn it at home every night until it becomes an essential part of your life. That's the value of writing it down.

You would be surprised at how few people actually put their vision in writing. There are even fewer who take the steps needed towards achieving it. Once broken down into small, achievable goals, even seemingly impossible dreams can be realized over time! I love what author James Allen said: "Your vision is the promise of what you shall one day be."

take action | NOW!

one: Find a vision that's right for you. Create a vision by asking yourself this question: What is my passion? What is it that excites me? Find your passion, and a powerful vision will follow.

two: Set yourself a big, imaginative, expansive vision. This will help to instil hope in the future for you and your staff.

three: Activate your vision. The Book of Habakkuk in the Old Testament instructs us to:
• Get the vision clear
• Write it down and make it succinct
• Say it out loud.

four: Start to visualize an exciting vision for your business right now. Capture it in your heart and in your mind.

two

MANAGE YOUR SUCCESS

Are you ready for what you are seeking?

"To build may have to be the slow and laborious task of years. To destroy can be the thoughtless act of a single day."
Sir Winston Churchill

Do you want a bigger business? Do you want more money? Do you want a larger house in a better suburb? Well what would happen if you suddenly got what you wanted? Would it change you for the better or for the worse?

For far too many people a sudden increase in wealth ruins their attitude, ruins their relationships, and ruins their business. The reason is that they never learned how to earn the wealth and they never learned how to manage it. I know of franchisees across different franchises who have a store with large sales and yet they still don't know how to manage their bills, they don't know how to pay their staff, and they don't even know how to treat people.

In the early years, a small number of franchisees began with Gloria Jean's Coffees after receiving an inheritance or winning the lottery or receiving a large severance package from work. We discovered that those franchisees often lost their money very quickly because they hadn't learned how to earn it, and they hadn't been through the tough decision-making times. I have found that, in most cases, if money comes easily it ruins people.

Sir Winston Churchill said, "To build may have to be the slow and laborious task of years. To destroy can be the thoughtless act of a single day." Have you ever noticed how lottery winners respond after winning a large prize? First there is the euphoria of winning. Then, within two or three years, there is nothing left. Their intentions were just to pay off the car loan or to go on an overseas holiday or to help their daughter buy a home. But they end up unable to manage the money and the family expectations. The resulting tension destroys relationships with family members and friends. The money is finally lost, wasted or fought over simply because they didn't earn it; they hadn't done the hard yards; they hadn't spent time building their business or their relationships. Someone once said, "How do you turn a big business into a small business? Give it to a small thinker!"

Small thinking limits growth

During my time in the advertising industry there were many occasions when two agencies merged to create one larger agency. But I noticed that within two years the size of that merged agency had diminished to the smaller size of each of the original pre-merged agencies. I discovered the reason for this: Those managing the newly merged agency were small thinkers used to managing smaller agencies. In normal day-to-day operations they would manage the business to the level they were familiar with. Their mindsets were more comfortable with the size of the agency they had come from. This meant the larger merged business would soon reduce to a size that was manageable for them. The size of their own small thinking limited the size of the business.

Professional hair stylist Vidal Sassoon once said, "The only place where success comes before work is in the dictionary." I often say to franchisees, "If this business was easy, everyone would be doing it!" When you buy into a franchise, the system is in place and, in most cases, has been tried and tested. It should be a simple case of franchisees following the directions of the franchisor. But there will always be hard work involved as well. In a franchise system you need to manage staff rosters, stock, bills, cleaning... You need to watch over that business. You can't simply sit back and expect it all to happen or you will not help your business to grow. You can't take your eyes off the business; if you do it will not give you the financial rewards you are looking for.

Chapter 13 in the Book of Proverbs in the Old Testament tells us that wealth gained easily or dishonestly will be diminished or will dwindle away, yet he who gathers by labour will increase his riches. God often gives us an idea which could potentially bring us success. That idea only becomes a reality when you set up a plan and you carry it out. Irish dramatist, literary critic and socialist George Bernard Shaw once stated:

People are always blaming circumstances for what they are. I do not believe in circumstance. The people who get on in this world are the people who get up and look for the circumstances they want, and if they cannot find them, make them.

Without a plan and execution, your seed will rot in the ground of excuses. Your gift or your idea is not to be put on display or wasted on worthless things or be denied out of a false sense of humility. It is to be invested, managed and developed. Its ultimate purpose is to bring reward and draw praise. Anything less than that is a waste of an idea.

Fear robs us of success

Be aware that fear is one of your greatest enemies. It numbs your spirit and hinders your creativity. Fear robs you of success. Fear tears down your dreams. If you don't use your talents, ideas and dreams you will lose them. You may think you're too old or you're too young. Wrong! There is no magical age at which excellence emerges or success suddenly comes knocking. You are never too young to realise your dreams and you are never too old for success. Thomas Jefferson was 33 when he drafted the Declaration of Independence. Michelangelo was painting some of his finest work at 87. Ray Kroc, the legend behind the Golden Arches, was introduced to McDonald's when he was 52. Colonel Sanders was at a ripe old age when he started Kentucky Fried Chicken. So learn to seize the day today and every day. Redeem the 'now' moments of your life while you can. The magical time you may be waiting for will likely never arrive.

Build a platform for long-term success

If you want more money, a bigger business, greater success in your current profession — if you want to see your dream realized — then start by building your groundwork now. How do you do that? Well here are some principles that will help you to build a platform for long-term success.

Relationships are fundamental. What is life without your family and friends? Build great relationships into your life that will encourage and challenge you. Make sure you learn from others who have been successful in this area. Learn what they did right and what they did wrong. That way you will eliminate a whole series of potential errors in your own life. Listen to those you respect when they challenge you about aspects of your relationships. There is nothing more valuable than the advice of a faithful friend when times are difficult.

Learn to manage well what you have now, even if you don't have much yet. The habits and attitudes you develop when you don't have much are critical to your future success. Those habits will determine how you respond when you gain more. Some people over-spend to achieve a desired lifestyle. Others adopt a miser-like attitude and keep their budget so tight that there is no room to enjoy life. Learn to balance your life and your finances so that you wisely tread the line between over-spending to enjoy life and being extremely tight so that you rarely enjoy life. Work hard to get your finances in order and keep regular track of your progress. It's amazing how many people fail in this basic step.

Learn to be generous. Do what you can to benefit others. It not only helps those you have helped, it has even more impact on your own life and outlook. Generosity, even in small ways, takes you outside your own problems. Generosity enlarges your thinking and your heart. It gives you tremendous motivation to succeed and it inspires others.

Generosity and open-heartedness attracts people to you. Others like to follow a generous leader. When a company invests into a charitable cause or program, it inspires the staff as well.

Over the years Gloria Jean's Coffees formed alliances with Mercy Ministries, Teen Challenge, Compassion, Opportunity International, the Salvation Army program for families in crisis, the Genes for Jeans campaign (providing funds for the Children's Medical Research Institute), and many other organizations and programs. As an organization we have sponsored 300 Compassion children in Brazil. We began with 200, and then staff and international Master Franchisees came on board. We worked alongside Opportunity International to provide microenterprise funding in third world countries. We found members of our support office team at Gloria Jean's Coffees so inspired by these projects that they voluntarily started fundraising and running team-building events to benefit our charity partners. Many invested in child sponsorship themselves. They not only enjoyed the giving aspect, they also had fun doing it.

Motivation to help grow the business increased when our staff saw that their hard work was benefiting the lives of others. Our international franchisors around the world have also decided to sponsor children and support Mercy Ministries. When you show leadership, your people get motivated. When you expand your thinking, your good people expand with you.

Be faithful with what is in your hand now. Jesus told a story in the New Testament about three men who were each given money to invest. The first two men doubled their money by investing wisely, but the third buried his coin in the ground because he was afraid to take a risk; he wanted to take the easy way out. This man was called a wicked, lazy servant. The lesson here is that we need to use what we have been given… or waste it. There is a risk both ways: You can risk the time and resources to use it, or risk the chance to lose it. The reward is in the investing.

Lastly, develop a large vision for every aspect of your life. That may be for your business, your relationships, your family, your finances or for you personally. A large vision is much more rewarding than a small vision. Then develop a plan to achieve the vision in stages. Start doing it now. Stop putting it off! If you're sick and tired of being sick and tired, then get started now.

take action |
NOW!

one: Recognise that relationships are fundamental to long-term success. Build valuable relationships with your family, friends and colleagues. These relationships will encourage and challenge you along your journey

two: Learn to manage well what you have now, even if you don't have much yet. The habits and attitudes you develop when you don't have much will determine how you respond when you gain more.

three: Be generous. Generosity enlarges your thinking and your heart. It gives you extra motivation to succeed.

four: Be faithful with what is in your hand now. If you don't use what you have been given, you run the risk of wasting it.

five: Develop a large vision for every aspect of your life: for your business, your relationships, your family, your finances or for you personally.

three |
ARE YOU IN A COMFORT ZONE?

Warning: Enlarge your vision or slip backwards

"Your successful past will block your visions of the future."
Joel A. Barker

Are you comfortable in your business or profession? Do you prefer to stay where you are? Do you feel like you don't want to be stretched any more? If you do, let me give you a word of warning: You are at a critical point at which complacency is likely to set in. In that comfort zone, your business or your job is likely to become stagnant. In fact, without forward momentum it could start slipping backwards.

I remember a managing director of the advertising agency I once worked for declaring that we should be very happy to get to billings of $10 million per annum and stay there. The agency was billing about AUD$7 million (USD$6 million) to AUD$8 million (almost USD$7 million) per annum at the time. Well, within one year we passed that target and went on to $14 million. And we continued to grow as the staff worked together on the renewed vision they had participated in formulating. In fact, if we'd stayed at $10 million, the agency would have died because inflation would not have covered the costs of running the agency at that time. On top of that, very few clients would have dealt with us because we would have been seen as virtually one of the smallest agencies in the country. When I left the agency, we had offices in all capital cities and the Sydney agency alone had grown to well over AUD$200 million (USD$172 million) in turnover. We were handling some very sizeable accounts and turning over healthy profits.

When we become comfortable in a business and even in a relationship, we begin to take it all for granted and we stop developing it. When that happens, we don't grow, so we need to challenge ourselves to expand our vision and stretch ourselves beyond our comfort zones. You need to ask yourself: Does your vision stretch you? The biggest obstacle we face in life and in business is small thinking and limited mindsets. The mindset in your business is normally set by the leaders or the owners of the business. If you are in a leadership position, throw out your small vision that is holding you to your comfort zone. Set a large vision, and then develop a plan to take on that vision in bite sizes over a period of time.

One of the biggest dangers for any business is the point at which you actually succeed in winning a large account or sales order. After many months of extra work and effort, long hours putting together presentations and submissions, you have finally done it! At that point, you will want to take a break. But this is probably one of the most dangerous and vulnerable times for your business. You and your staff will tend to settle back and become comfortable, but be warned that if you do that the business will lose momentum and stop growing. In fact, not only will you probably mishandle the new business, you may also start to lose other orders or other business… all because of complacency!

Instead, after winning a major client or sales account, your business needs to keep moving forward. In fact, at that important time in the life of your business, the leader of your business (whether that is you or your boss) needs to be able to regenerate and restructure the whole company.

Constantly review your company structure

When I was managing director at DDB Needham Advertising, and even during my time with Gloria Jean's Coffees, whenever we put a new company structure in place the question most commonly asked was: "How long do you think this structure will last?" Now, at that time everyone would naturally expect the structure to suit us for at least two years; then we would have outgrown that model. However, when facing this question, I always say jokingly, "About two weeks!"

I believe a company structure and a business should constantly be under review. If a company is growing—even if it is a small growth—there will need to be constant reviews of the structure to take into account the way the company has developed. After we purchased the international rights for Gloria Jean's Coffees, we put into place a strong sales development team to sell Master Franchise rights for different countries. We were bringing so many countries on board that we soon realized our structure had become irrelevant. We also needed to operationally support the new franchisees around the world as they opened their stores in their countries.

When we had only 30 Gloria Jean's Coffees stores in Australia, the structure to support this size was totally different to the one we have today to support over 400 stores. The support structures and systems operate at a totally different level to the way they did when we started. We had prepared a business plan and a structure for our international growth, but as we were signing up considerably more countries (and many of these countries were beginning to open more stores than their original plans), we had to revise our company structure to meet and support that need. If you are not continually revisiting your structure to meet new needs, then your whole company can easily stagnate and even go backwards to the point of collapse.

Continually enlarge your vision

Life is a journey, not a destination. Whether it's a major business, a small business or a retail business, you haven't arrived at success the day you open your business. Neither have you arrived the day you get married, the day you join a sporting team, or the day you win a major achievement award. At these points in your life, your journey is only just starting. There will still be obstacles, difficulties and mountains to climb. There will still be new lessons to learn and changes to make. Disappointments and challenges, celebrations and cheers will continue to greet you throughout your whole life. So you will need to continually stretch and enlarge your thinking. You will need to regularly develop an expansive attitude. The prophet Isaiah in the Old Testament wrote:

Enlarge the place of your tent, stretch your tent curtains wide, do not hold back; lengthen your cords, strengthen your stakes. For you will spread out to the right and to the left; your descendants will dispossess nations... (Isaiah 54:2)

Are you getting ready for where you want your business to be? Are you preparing to achieve your new, enlarged vision? It is critically important to get ready for growth in your business. You need to be thinking ahead. Every decision you make regarding infrastructure, equipment and systems needs to be a base model that is able to grow, develop and expand to satisfy the growth you plan for your business.

Little did we know when we started Gloria Jean's Coffees in Australia—and we originally planned for 25 stores to be opened over a ten-year term—that we would have well over 300 stores by the time we got to the tenth year. Today we have over 400 stores in Australia. Little did we know that we would take up an opportunity to buy the brand internationally and supply franchise rights for the world. That wasn't part of our early vision, but an enlarged vision creates new opportunities.

Our vision, although it was large, certainly stretched our thinking and opened our hearts and minds to new possibilities. As we started to grow, the vision didn't change but expanded to cover more stores. Then it expanded further when the international opportunity came onto the agenda.

Little did we know when we launched in Australia that within a few years we would be able to provide significant support to a charity called Mercy Ministries. We always wanted to be able to support the community in significant ways, and Mercy Ministries became our opportunity to do that. Mercy Ministries is still our main focus, but today we are also supporting Compassion by sponsoring children in a coffee growing region of Brazil. We are also supporting Opportunity International, which provides low interest loans to people in third world countries so they can start businesses, enhancing their lives and local economies. We are also proud supporters of Teen Challenge, which runs programs for young men overcoming drug and alcohol dependency.

Our partnership with Mercy Ministries gave us the opportunity to put cash donation boxes in our stores alongside leaflets explaining what Mercy Ministries is all about. This has not only raised much-needed funds to run the Mercy Ministries homes, it has also raised awareness of the needs of young women in our community and the help Mercy Ministries provides for these young women. Even more exciting to us personally is the opportunity we now have to take this alliance overseas as both Mercy Ministries and Gloria Jean's Coffees expands internationally. The Mercy Ministries home in the United Kingdom has already opened with enthusiastic support from our English franchise partners. Over the next 12 months other countries are in the planning stages of this special alliance.

I have seen many businesses grow and expand and I would like to see yours do the same. So step out of your comfort zone, enlarge your vision, and establish plans to realize your goals.

take action | NOW!

one: If you have a small vision that is holding you back, throw it out now

two: Establish a larger vision that will stretch you beyond your comfort zone

three: Develop a plan to progress towards your enlarged vision in bite sizes over a period of time

four: Constantly review your company structure...
        remain flexible to allow for change as you grow.

four |

CHALLENGES

"You gain strength, courage and confidence by every experience in which you really stop to look fear in the face. You are able to say to yourself, 'I have lived through this horror. I can take the next thing that comes along.' You must do the thing you think you cannot do."
Eleanor Roosevelt

Some of us tend to believe that successful people in business, media, politics and sport have always been winners. We think they don't know what it's like to go through tough times like the rest of us. If you believe that, then allow me to destroy that myth. The fact is that everyone faces challenges, but successful people learn to break through them.

People have often said to me, "It's easy for you — you own a large business with a large turnover and many stores. People will listen to you!" They forget that a large business starts off as a small business. Ten years ago no one knew who Gloria Jean's Coffees was. We had people who didn't want to work for us. We had people who didn't want to supply products to us. When we started Gloria Jean's Coffees we were told, "We don't want to supply you because you won't amount to anything!" Because we were small, we had trouble negotiating good prices and getting the supplies we needed from the United States.

We've come a long way since then. What is a small amount of money to us today was a lot of money back then. During the early years cash flow was always an issue. In many cases those difficulties haven't changed, they've simply escalated! These days the numbers just have more noughts on the end! It's all relative as you grow larger.

In response to a newspaper headline declaring 'Innocent Bystander Shot in New York', American humorist and movie actor Will Rogers once stated: "You just stand around in this town long enough and be innocent and somebody's gonna shoot ya." That's how it is with challenges; just stand by and you'll get hit. In both business and life there will always be trials that surprise us out of nowhere, and they will be different every time. My attitude to this is: We're going through life, we're learning, we're growing, and we will deal with those difficulties as they arise.

It's tough when you start a business. No one said there wouldn't be obstacles, difficulties and daunting decisions to be made. When you are growing your business, the decisions you will have to make are not always going to be easy. You'll always be investing time and money into the business. There will be many times when staff will need to leave you because they are more of a hindrance than a help. Even today we encounter people who don't like our vision, mission and values and who don't want to join our company. It's better to find that out before they start, because if they join you they are not going to be committed to your vision, mission and values.

In business, tough decisions mean the pressure can mount. You don't want to get into the situation in which John Paul Getty, one of the wealthiest people in the US, found himself when he said, "I have so much money I can buy every heifer in the United States but my stomach is so full of ulcers I cannot even enjoy one steak." When you see yourself heading into that situation, you need to get help. You should try to read the signs beforehand and then start talking to people who can help you.

When we reach a critical stage in which we begin to experience high pressure, we don't make good business decisions. I've learned to avoid making difficult or important decisions when I am tired or under severe stress. In times of crisis, decisions still need to be made, but leave the major or life-changing ones until you have a clear mind.

For those of you who are committed in your faith, you need to learn to hand these situations to God. At these times we need to look for someone who is going to give us wise advice. Someone outside the situation you are facing can give objective advice without the emotional attachment. Look for positive, worthwhile advice. Avoid those people who will tell you the situation is hopeless. Steer clear of those who are looking at the problem instead of the solution, the potential or the opportunities.

Every challenge serves a purpose

Every challenge serves a purpose... if you don't allow it to overcome you. A challenge can even become an opportunity. Albert Einstein once stated, "In the middle of difficulty lies opportunity." Through challenges, you learn and become better prepared for the next stage of your life and your business growth. And sometimes it's not just about you. Every challenge you've had to overcome should also serve as an encouragement to someone else. The trials you have overcome can serve as valuable experience to help others either avoid or triumph over those same trials.

Stop focusing on your weaknesses and limitations and appreciate and draw on your strengths. Everyone has strengths. Learn to use them more. If you focus too much on your weakness, you'll become weaker. The danger in analyzing your situation too much is that you can drown in your own defeat. Avoid over-analysis and stop trying to compare yourself with others. Just be yourself. People are drawn to you because you are you. Your friends know your strengths and that warms them to you.

It helps to be reminded that crises and challenges do not last forever. Speaker and author Jerry Savelle said, "A financial crisis is not permanent. It is subject to change. Sickness and disease are not permanent. They are subject to change." You may be in a season of sowing right now. It's hard work and you can't see the rewards. Well, just as any farmer knows, the season of harvest will come again.

Today you may be facing an impossible situation. It may seem that there is no way out for you. You may feel desperate and defeated. But don't give up! Walt Disney once declared, "It's kind of fun to do the impossible." He should know! I once heard that over 190 banks knocked him back before one bank agreed to help finance his Disney World venture.

Leaders enjoy challenges

Whether you are in business or not, you are in one of these three stages right now: You are either in a trial, coming out of a trial, or heading towards the next trial. This just happens to be a way of life. There is always some difficulty to face, but true business people and real leaders enjoy the challenge of solving problems.

Often someone will approach me with a problem but with no solution. They'll believe they are at a dead end. When you sit with them and analyse their situation, you soon determine that there are many ways to tackle their problem. At this advice, their eyes open wide. They hadn't realised that there were so many options to resolving the matter.

Today, through the growth of our business, there are many issues we faced in the early days that we now brush aside. Back then, these challenges had the potential to knock us over. Today we have bigger issues to face that have the potential to knock us down. We've simply got to learn to get up, learn to do battle, and learn to deal with them. Difficulties, problems and issues will produce maturity in us. I don't know of any other way that you are going to grow other than to work your way through the challenges.

Challenges motivate action

Author and motivational speaker Zig Ziglar likes to tell the following story. A gentleman who worked on the 4pm-to-midnight shift walked home after work every night. One night the moon was shining so brightly that he decided to take a shortcut through the cemetery, shaving roughly a kilometre off his walk. He found no difficulties along the route that night, so he repeated the process on a regular basis, always following the same path.

One night, as he was walking through the cemetery, he didn't realise that during the day a grave had been freshly dug in the centre of his path. He fell right into the open grave. Desperately he tried to climb out, but his best efforts failed. After a few minutes he decided to relax and wait until the morning when someone would help him out. He sat down in a corner and was half asleep when a drunk stumbled into the grave. His arrival roused the first man, since the drunk was desperately trying to climb out, clawing frantically at the sides. Our hero reached out his hand, touched the drunk on the leg, and said, "Friend, you can't get out of here." But he did! Now that's motivation!

A visit to your local cemetery at night may be just the thing you need to help you re-evaluate and re-prioritize your life... to make the rest of your life the best of your life!

During the last two years of my advertising career, I had taken over as managing director of the advertising agency and we were growing strongly. We had built a strong vision for the future and everything seemed to be tracking well. These are the times in which you think there is never going to be another major problem that can hit you. But all it takes is a phone call from your client who says he's going to review your business. A significant client can cause a large impact. Then, as you prepare for the presentation and you are waiting for the client to come in, you receive a call from another client who says he wants to review your business. In both instances, we kept those clients, but that experience made the agency sharper. It re-energized our staff and it re-focused us on better servicing our existing clients. You learn through these challenging periods.

Challenges grow us

We have faced many issues at Gloria Jean's Coffees. There are times when a small number of franchisees believe that no one is helping them. They blame their accountant, suppliers, staff and even the support office at Gloria Jean's Coffees. They make everyone's life difficult, including their own. The expectation is that when they open the door to their store it should all just happen for them with no work required. When you sit with them and work your way through the situation, there is often a misunderstanding or an incorrect expectation and you begin building a new relationship. Most of us would prefer that none of these situations happen, but without that kind of challenge real growth may never happen.

Franchisees themselves experience a variety of hardships. There have been instances when someone has broken into a store at night and stolen the safe. There have been times when a customer, for whatever reason, has become really difficult to deal with. In fact, these few customers are generally known to be difficult in other retail outlets. You need to make sure that these rare, difficult customers do not kill your vision, do not kill your passion, and do not kill your dream.

It's easy to take to heart the insults or criticisms from customers. It's easy to become emotionally affected and lose perspective, especially when you are people-focussed in your business. However, learn to smile and ride above the criticism with grace. Your remaining customers will appreciate it. And you'll feel better for it.

Once we realise that we are on a journey, that we can climb the mountains before us, that we can plough through the walls of difficulties, and that we can soar like eagles over the peaks of challenges, then we start to appreciate life. Then we can begin to enjoy the journey... and the challenges.

take action |
NOW!

one: Realise that right now every one of us is in one of these three stages: in a trial, coming out of a trial, or heading towards the next trial.

two: Learn to stand up and deal with your challenges.

three: Avoid over-analysis of your situation and stop trying to compare yourself with others.

four: Avoid making difficult or important decisions when you are tired or under severe stress.

five: Take your eyes off your weaknesses and focus on your strengths. Learn to use your strengths more.

six: List all the solutions available to you and work your way through them.

seven: If you are committed to your faith, learn to hand your challenging situation to God.

eight: Learn to enjoy the challenge of solving problems.

nine: Use the challenges to re-energize and re-focus yourself and the people around you.

five

STAY ON COURSE

When challenges get in your way

"You can't drive through life looking in the rear view mirror."
Terri Savelle Foy

About 12 months ago, while Sue and I were on holidays, we watched a very old movie called *The Gumball Rally*. It's about an automobile race from the east coast to the west coast of the USA. There are no rules and the first car to arrive at the finish line wins the race. A variety of characters enter this race. Some take part for the social aspect; they just want to enjoy the journey. But most of the drivers are very competitive and attempt to win the race at any cost. After much preparation and excitement, two of the stars jump into a sports car as the race is about to start. One of them grabs the rear view mirror, rips it off, throws it onto the back seat and declares, "And now my friend, the first rule of Italian driving: Whatsa behind me is not important!"

When Sue and I heard that statement, it struck a chord with both of us. We have always believed that in life you need to learn from the past so that you can grow, but you can't keep looking back or you will never go forward. It's easy to say, "If only we were back in the 'good old days'!" But if you really think back to the 'good old days', they weren't that good anyway! Life wasn't as easy back then as it can be today. We didn't have all the things that make life a lot better today, such as employment opportunities, variety of sports, education for self improvement, medical innovations and entertainment. Sue and I have learned a lot of lessons from the past that enable us to tackle many issues today.

We've learned from the past, but we recognize that we need to keep looking forward.

It's not strange that in your car you have a small rear vision mirror facing backwards and you have a very wide windscreen facing forward. The wide windscreen is what is before you and what is behind you is very narrow. What this tells us is that you can learn from the past, but if you keep looking back you will lose momentum. If you keep looking back, your competitors will pass you. If you keep looking back, you'll get run over!

In Disney's *The Lion King*, Rafikki gave this advice to young Simba: "The way I see it, you can either run from it, or learn from it." You should never regret or ignore lessons learned from the past, because life is a journey. The past may appear to be better viewed after the event, but even if you could go back in time, the experience would never live up to your memory of it. Your future—your vision—is part of that wide windscreen ahead of you.

Keep moving forward

We need to keep looking forward in our business and in our relationships. We can't keep looking back at our competition and continually regretting our mistakes. Often when we face problems or difficulties (that appear like mountains), we tend to turn around and look back, but we need to keep looking forward to be able to plough through those problems (those mountains). You've heard the saying, "The definition of insanity is to keep doing the same thing in the same way while expecting a different result." Continually looking back only makes us want to do the same thing in the same way.

When we started on the Gloria Jean's Coffees journey, we set about looking forward. We set about planning the future, we set about working towards the vision, and we set about creating the category we were going to become successful in. We were going to be different, and yet we soon discovered that many competitors and other retail concepts started to follow us. When we introduced a new product or concept, we discovered that we had at least two or three years lead over our copycat competitors. Today, in many instances it's only a matter of a few months before people start copying. The gap has narrowed.

Any business is a risk, but I have found that if you look back too much then you create a bigger risk. In the Old Testament, the Israelites under Moses' leadership never made it to the Promised Land (only their descendants did) because their desire had been to return to Egypt where they came from and where they thought they were comfortable. But back in Egypt they had struggled to survive under slavery and oppression. Because they looked back, they missed out on a better place, a prosperous place, and a more successful place—all because they didn't want to take the risk and face the challenges ahead.

Sometimes it's tough looking ahead; all you can see are the challenges and the hard times. But remember that looking back won't help you either. If you are under attack in your business, if you are under attack from your competitors, enjoy the compliment! If you are taking ground, then somebody's losing ground and they won't like it! Part of succeeding in business is facing some competition. As the saying goes, "No pain, no gain."

I have developed a business and mentoring relationship with Jason Berry, the General Manager of Brisbane community radio station 96.5 FM (in Queensland, Australia). This station has a limited licence compared to the major commercial radio stations in the market. Through positioning the station with a family focus, embracing community care and innovation, Jason and his team have built a very successful station. Many of the marketing, promotional and community care activities have achieved a sizeable listening audience. Some competing stations in the market have criticised the station, written letters against the station, and verbally 'bad-mouthed' the station. They have even resorted to reporting them to the Australian Broadcasting Authority which issues the radio licences. They have failed to close the station or slow its progress, as 96.5 FM operates correctly within its licence parameters. I have encouraged Jason to enjoy the compliment and keep innovating to lift the bar for this industry. The competing stations have far more resources and less advertising restrictions, but they keep looking at the competition instead of the resources they have at their disposal.

Futurist Leon Martel says we can all become guilty of three common traps that can prevent us from pursuing our vision:

1. Believing that yesterday's solutions will overcome today's problems
2. Assuming that present trends will continue
3. Neglecting the opportunities offered by the future.
   Beware of the trap in believing that current ideas, thoughts, procedures, teachings and communication methods will continue in the same way in the future. If you fall into that trap, you will risk missing out on opportunities that present themselves in the future. It's worth investing in resources such as books and journals that help you regularly take a peek into future trends and issues and that also expand your thinking. Who knows, you may discover a whole new range of products or services that will catapult you to another level of success! Opportunities tend to fall into the path of people who look forward rather than backward.

Stay focused

The way to stay on course in your business is to stay focused. Focused people are not easily distracted. Focused people refuse to compromise on what they believe. Focused people will not compromise on their passion. Focused people will make no provision for failure. Focused people do not change what they believe because of circumstances. And focused people finish what they start.

If there is one thing that will keep you on course through the hard times, it's passion. Passion will give you strength to run through walls of opposition. It will sustain you over the long haul. Without passion you will struggle to maintain momentum when obstacles try to slow you down. How strong is your passion for your business? If your passion is weak, you won't get very far. If your passion is weak, even minor problems will distract you from your vision. The success of your business requires that the level of your passion remains consistently strong. Passion overcomes distractions.

There are many distractions that drag us off course. So often we are dragged off course by friends, family and others who have the right intentions and who want to offer us 'good' advice. But sometimes their advice sends us in the wrong direction. Ultimately you have the choice to listen to or ignore their advice.

At other times our own mistakes can drag us off course. Failure is just another way to more intelligently start all over again. We all make mistakes, but some of us stop and turn back at that point, while others pick themselves up and keep going. When you face these potential distractions, you need to call it the way you see it. You will always make mistakes and you will need to seek help, but in the end you have the vision. It's your vision, so it's your call as to what you do when you are tempted to steer off course. It's your call whether you give up or continue on your course.

The Book of Proverbs in the Old Testament says, "Plans fail for lack of counsel". (Proverbs 15:22) When making decisions it pays to get advice, but be careful where you get it. So often we surround ourselves with people who provide advice—such as friends, family and business associates—yet quite often these people provide negative advice by simply telling us what can't be done. They often seem to have a better idea than the one we have in our heart and the one we have put to paper. So call it the way you see it. It's your vision, not theirs.

You can also seek advice from books. It seems that there is a book for every problem under the sun. But not all books are helpful. Often they are written by people who haven't actually done what they talk about. They've done the talking without the walking. Read books written by people who have 'been there, done that'.

Whenever you make a decision to do something, whether it is to launch a product, grow a product, expand a business or give money away, you will find there will be people who will oppose you or disagree with you. Research in the USA has found that ten percent of people will disagree with what you are doing. You cannot build a business based on that ten percent. They will not be loyal to you. They will be critical and they will move onto the next product, service or business that comes along... and they will continue to criticize. Instead, you need to build the business on those people who are going to become your customers. If we had listened to that ten percent of people in the early days of Gloria Jean's Coffees, our business would not be here today.

Don't always listen to customers

When we started in Australia, people told us that flavoured coffees, takeaway cups and a lack of table service would not work. They said that customers in Australia were used to sitting down with table service, drinking coffee from a crockery mug, paying for it at the end, and often ordering a coffee with their meal. We didn't listen to these people and today we have a large prospering business! In fact, the whole coffee industry is now significantly greater than what it was when we started... because we didn't listen to that ten percent. Back then the coffee industry was actually stagnant and people only sat down for a coffee outside their home on special occasions, to meet a friend, or after a meal.

We have actually now seen a total lifestyle and mindset change. Today, drinking coffee outside the home is an everyday occurrence. In fact, we've changed the whole mindset of the way people drink tea or coffee. And we've changed the whole mindset of the way people socialise. By providing a safe, warm and inviting place to meet people with great coffee and other beverages, while offering lots of variety and a friendly service, we caught the trend in what people actually wanted (even though it was an unexpressed need at that time).

In fact, our concept and the specialist coffee industry that we operate in is now seen as a lifestyle concept. This has been driven by coffee-drinking actors in movies and TV sitcom programs like Frasier, Seinfeld and Friends, which run not only in Australia and the USA but in many countries around the world. Even in their own language people see the stars sitting and socialising in a comfortable environment around a cup of coffee. The media industry has picked up coffee drinking as a desirable lifestyle so that now you see images of people meeting in coffee shops or people drinking lattes featuring in many advertisements. Posters promoting property, shopping centres and resorts depict people relaxing over coffee. Many businesses attempt to attract customers with the lure of a great cappuccino or latte in prestige car showrooms, upmarket beauticians and hair salons, bookstores and garden nurseries. These businesses now include an espresso machine or a coffee shop area on their premises.

When you deliver a great product like Gloria Jean's Coffees, you need to have all the elements working together—the atmosphere, the ambience, the location, the lifestyle and great customer interaction—so that you can build a great business. Without these elements we would not be doing the transactions we see in our stores today.

As I have mentioned before, a former CEO of Sony Corporation once said, "We don't do any consumer research on product development. The customer has no idea what we are capable of – only we know that – so we make new products and then educate the consumer on why they should have those products." If Sony had believed its product development research back then, you would not see Walkman or PlayStation products on shelves today (and that might have been a good thing). Back then, Sony's customers could not have imagined Walkman or PlayStation inventions. They only wanted larger colour TV screens and better sound systems.

Customers do not know what you are capable of in your business in terms of your product or your service. You need to believe in yourself and have a passion for your product or service… then go out and excite your potential and existing customers. You need to say to yourself, "If it's going to be, it's up to me!"

Believe in yourself

I like this quote from Virgil, of the most influential Roman authors throughout history: "They can because they think they can." Perhaps you don't know what you are capable of. If so, then you need to sit down and look at your business. You need to develop your future plan and your vision based on where you believe you can go. You have to believe in yourself and believe in your product. If you don't, you might as well give up because you aren't going to go anywhere. No one is going to buy from someone who isn't passionate and committed to their product or service.

In the end, you have to lead; no one else can build your business for you. The character of Lieutenant Colonel Henry Blake—the commanding officer in the long-running TV series MASH—was always deferring leadership decisions. When he was under pressure, he always looked for someone else to make that decision. In the end, the buck stops with you. You need to realise that anyone else who gets involved with recommendations and ideas won't necessarily have your passion. You need to listen to advice, you need to make changes, but you still need to be committed to the vision and plan that you have set in place.

Nehemiah, a prophet in the Old Testament, could see a problem: The need to rebuild the defensive wall around Jerusalem. He could even see the solution. In fact, he saw both the problem and the solution without ever visiting Jerusalem itself. That's why he received approval from the king to rebuild the wall. That's an incredible characteristic of a great leader: The ability to discern the problem from a distance, to see the solution, to take the initiative (and the risk), and to complete the task.

Author John Maxwell said that Nehemiah could see further than others, more than others, and he could see what was needed before others could see it. Nehemiah knew the wall could and should be rebuilt, and he knew what it would take to rebuild it. Before he left for Jerusalem, he asked the king for letters of authorisation allowing him to gather materials to be able to finish the task. None of Jerusalem's neighbours wanted the wall rebuilt. Nehemiah knew this and prepared strategies to counter their opposition. He could see the opposition before it materialised. The result was that Nehemiah led a team of people to rebuild the massive city wall in just 52 days! They were able to do it because

they had a great leader to navigate for them.
But before the rebuilding process began, Nehemiah:

1.   Identified the problem
2.   Spent time in prayer
3.   Approached key influencers
4.   Assessed the situation
5.   Met with the people and cast the vision
6.   Encouraged the people with past successes
7.   Received buy-in from the people
8.   Organised the people and got them working.

That's a great checklist for you and your business as well. Nehemiah's checklist can help set you on the right course.

Have a 'can do' attitude

Author and speaker Chuck Swindoll said, "I believe the single most significant decision I can make on a day-to-day basis is my choice of attitude. When my attitudes are right, there is no barrier too high, no valley too deep, no dream too extreme, no challenge too great for me." An attitude like that is important to have because there will be friends and associates who will present you with many reasons why you can't do something. At times a staff member would come to me and say, "We've got an impossible situation!" They don't any more, because my response is always to sit and review the details of the problem and to find solutions. They soon realise that there are always options before them. I believe there are always solutions to any problem.

Some of your initial ideas may not be the best solutions to your problem, but your initial ideas extend your thinking and extend the boundaries, and great solutions end up coming your way. Learn to have a 'can do' attitude. The solution may not come immediately, but it will come. And the more solutions that come your way in the long run will ultimately define your long-term success.

The story is told of President Thomas Jefferson and a group of companions who travelled across the country on horseback. They came to a river that had overflowed its bank because of a recent downpour. The river had washed away the bridge, so each rider was forced to cross on horseback. Each time they crossed that river they fought for their lives against the current. A stranger stopped on the bank to watch. After several riders had plunged into the river and made it to safety on the other side, the stranger turned to President Jefferson and asked if he would carry him across on his horse. The President agreed without hesitation. So the man climbed onto the President's horse and the two of them crossed the raging torrents to the other side. As the stranger slid off the horse onto dry ground, one of President Jefferson's companions asked him, "Why did you select the President to help you across the river?" Initially the man was shocked that it was the President who had helped him cross the river. "All I know," he said, "is that on some of your faces was written the answer 'No' and on some the answer 'Yes'. The President had a 'Yes' face."

A good attitude has a 'Yes' face. Do you have a 'Yes' face? Your attitude will determine your success.

So stay the vision; stay on course. When problems seem insurmountable, when obstacles stop you dead in your tracks, take counsel from the right people—from people with a 'Yes' face—and keep moving forward. Your focus and your passion will carry the momentum for you as you circumnavigate the challenges.

take action |
NOW!

one: Regularly invest in resources (such as books, magazines and CDs) that help you peek into future trends and issues.

two: Learn to discern problems from a distance, recognise the solutions, and take the initiative (and the risk) to activate your solutions.

three: Adopt a 'can do' attitude.

four: Believe in yourself and believe in your product.

five: Stay focused and passionate.

six: Keep moving forward – don't look back for long.

seven: Don't always listen to your customers.

eight: Follow Nehemiah's check-list:
- Identify the problem
- Spend time in prayer
- Approach key influencers
- Assess the situation
- Meet with key people and cast the vision
- Encourage the people with past successes
- Receive buy-in from the people
- Organise the people and get them working.

six

PEOPLE

"It is important people believe in their leader, but it is more important that the leader believes in his people."
John Maxwell

The human body contains many parts, such as arms, legs, eyes, nose, mouth, ears... Each one has a specific role to play to keep the whole body functioning successfully. In the same way, a team of people is made up of many parts, and each person has a role to fulfill. This is true within a company or a store or a charity. If one person does not function properly, then the whole team feels the effect.

There is a great story told about Jimmy Durante, one of the truly great entertainers. He was asked to do a show for World War II veterans. He told them he was very busy, but if they wouldn't mind him doing one short monologue and immediately leaving for his next appointment, he'd come. The organisers agreed.

At the appointed time and day, Jimmy arrived and stepped onto the stage. He performed his short monologue, but then he stayed... and stayed. Soon he'd been on stage 15, 20, then 30 minutes. Finally he took a last bow and left. Backstage, someone stopped him and said, "I thought you had to go after a few minutes. What happened?"

Jimmy answered, "You can see for yourself—look in the front row."
In the front row were two World War II veterans, each of whom

had lost an arm in the war. One had lost his right arm and the other had lost his left arm. Together they were able to clap in time, and that's exactly what they were doing... loudly and cheerfully. That's why Jimmy had stayed.

In your own team, you will have some people with strengths in one area and others who are weak in that same area. That's great, because they can complement each other. Some are great at supervising teams, others are great at managing budgets, and still others are creative geniuses. We're all members of a team and we all pull together to help each other for a cause, such as the business you work in.

You yourself may have blind spots in which you can't see everything going on in your business. But if you have someone on your team who has 20/20 vision, then you need their counsel. There will be others on your team who have qualities you don't have, and you must be open to seeking their correction, comfort and fellowship... and they also need yours. That's what needs to happen in a business and in a team-working environment. Together you and your people make a powerful team. Like the World War II veterans, it's exciting to see members of your team clapping hands together. Is your business like that?

One way to build team spirit is to believe in your people and help them believe in themselves. People often rise to the level of the encouragement they receive. Author and leadership expert John Maxwell once said, "It is important people believe in their leader, but it is more important that the leader believes in his people." Believe in them, encourage them, and they will follow you.

Leading people through change

Moses in the Old Testament was a great leader of people. He got his people to do amazing things! In *The Maxwell Leadership Bible*, John Maxwell quotes management consultant Peter Drucker, who helps us learn from Moses about how to lead people into change. In this book he talks about the 'law of buy-in':
1. *Magnify the plagues:* To make Pharaoh release God's people, Moses called down the plagues, and he didn't stop until the old

system gave way. At this stage, problems are your friend. Don't solve them; they convince people that they need to let go of the old way." Once you solve the problems for them, then people stay where they are; they don't see the need to change.

2. **Mark the ending:** What a symbolic and memorable 'boundary event' Moses had in crossing the Red Sea! After the people walked through the waters on dry land there was no turning back." We need to make sure our people know the point at which they have crossed over the line of definite change. They then need to realize that there is no opportunity to go back to the past.

3. **Deal with the murmuring:** Don't be surprised when some lose confidence in your leadership somewhere between where they came from and where they're going. Moses heard things like 'Does our leader know the way? We've never done it this way before. What was so bad back in Egypt?'" Be prepared for the rumours. Realize that your team will question your authority. Stand up as a leader. Do your people see your can-do attitude? Do they recognize your leadership qualities?

4. **Give people access to decision makers:** Thanks to Jethro, Moses appointed a new cadre of leaders to narrow the gap between the people and the decision makers. As a result the people felt more connected." If your door is always closed and you are never available, your people will become disconnected from you and from the vision. Your PA, General Manager or Office Manager will then become the de-facto leader of your organisation. They will make decisions for you, second guess your decisions, or criticize you and/ or become over protective of you. So remove the barricades and get involved again.

5. **Capitalise on the creative opportunity of the wilderness:** It was in the wilderness, not the Promised Land, that a big innovation took place. God handed down the ten commandments. Some of your biggest breakthroughs will also take place in the wilderness." Make the most of your wilderness experience. You are more likely to make innovative and revolutionary decisions in the tough times.

6. **Resist the urge to rush ahead:** It often seems that little happens

in the wilderness, but great transformation takes place there. Don't jeopardize it by hurrying ahead or removing the pain of giving birth to a new vision. Let God do this work." Value your tough times, for they will prepare you and mould you into a better person and a more effective leader.

7. *Understand that wilderness leadership is special:* Moses did not enter the Promised Land. His kind of leadership fitted the transition time, where things seemed confusing and fluid. The nation needed Joshua to enter Canaan, because he led the military, and because a settled life required new skills. Movements and organizations don't always need a new leader; but they do require a new style of leadership once the transition is complete." Joshua was a strong, courageous, military leader; he was the right man for this new job. The new life required new skills and a different leadership style. Do you possess the right leadership style for your organisation right now?

The lesson here is this: If your organization is going through change and transition—a kind of wilderness experience—then you will need to recognize the qualities that are needed to lead your team through this unique phase. So set your vision and begin the journey.

Passion, commitment and enthusiasm

One of the greatest qualities to have in a team environment is passion. Every team needs people with passion, commitment and enthusiasm. Whether you are an employer or employee, ask yourself this question: Do you have passion, commitment and enthusiasm in your role? Author and speaker Keith Abraham, in his book *Inspirational Insights*, says, "Life is not about pursuing your passion one day, it's about having a passion every day." Don't become like the people American educator, publicist and political figure, Nicholas Murray Butler, spoke about when he said: "Many people's tombstones should read, 'Died at 30, buried at 60.'" Instead, live and work every day as though it is your first day! President and COO of The Ritz-Carlton Hotel Company, Horst Schultze, once said:
You are nothing unless it comes from your heart. Passion, caring,

really looking to create excellence... If you perform functions only and go to work only to do processes, then you have effectively retired. And it scares me — most people I see by age 28 are retired. If you go to work only to fulfill the processes of functions — then you are a machine. You have to bring passion, commitment and caring, that's what makes you a human being.

We are not here on this earth just to get by and to pay bills. If you are here to work, pay bills and simply survive, then what a waste of a life!

Today we are fortunate that we have many choices of jobs that can cater to our passions. You and I have the opportunity to get involved in almost any industry that involves something we may be passionate about. You can buy a franchise, develop your own business, or apply for a job in an industry that actually suits your desires and skills. Why waste your time in a job or an industry that you don't enjoy and in which you don't get to use your skills? And even if your current job is not exactly where you want to be, work with a positive attitude, commit to it with a passion, and start planning ahead for a change for the better. You will soon find that there is something to learn from every situation in life that will move you towards your dreams.

Staff who embrace the vision

At Gloria Jean's Coffees we are still resolving issues created from hiring the wrong people. I have learned from experience that you need people who are going to embrace the vision. You need people who are committed to where you want to go. I remember a few years ago we wanted to open 100 new stores within a 12 month period. When we announced this to our staff, some of them went white. In the end, we never achieved the goal of 100 stores in one year. We failed not because it wasn't possible — other retail franchise companies have been able to achieve this result — it was because of the mindsets, body language and actions of some of our people. Their lack of enthusiasm and commitment actually 'cannibalized' our opportunity. They didn't deliberately set out to stop us achieving our goal, but their small-thinking limitations and their comfort zones actually hindered our growth.

At eight minutes past midnight on October 3, 2002, my wife and I received a phone call from our security people to inform us that our warehouse was on fire. My wife answered the phone (I'm not exactly firing on all cylinders at that time of night). I remember saying to her, "Thank goodness I'm dreaming!"

"You're not dreaming!" she was quick to tell me.

As I slid out of bed and got dressed, I remembered what my mother had once said to me: "Always be prepared!" So I decided I wouldn't just put a coat over my pyjamas; I would get fully dressed, just in case...

On the way to the warehouse my wife and I prayed, rather urgently. When we arrived we saw two fire engines and one local journalist. There appeared to be a trickle of smoke rising through the roof. At that point I thought perhaps most of our stock would be safe... until the firemen cut their way through the roller shutters and we saw the inferno inside! Within an hour the blaze was horrific! In fact, the building and stock would continue to burn for three days.

Fire at Gloria Jean's Coffees attracts media

By the morning there were 31 fire engines and a small army of fire fighters. The smoke and the trucks blocked one of our busiest local roads. Burned coffee and debris polluted the nearby creek, and locals several blocks away had their yards covered in ash. Gloria Jean's Coffees quickly became not only top-of-mind in the local community that day, but also top-of-mind nationally through extensive media coverage. Footage of our burning warehouse was broadcast on television news channels across the nation.

Sitting in the car park away from the fire, I asked God, "What will we do?!" At that stage we had 92 stores and had hired a whole team of staff. I remember clearly the following response, "Well, you have your green (unroasted) coffee beans and your cups and lids stored off-site, so you can always fly product in." On the advice of the Fire Chief we returned home. He told us there was nothing we could do at the site.

At 5:30 that morning I returned to the burning warehouse and office because I wanted to arrive before the roasting team and warehouse staff who always started work early. When they arrived I told them, "There is nothing for you to do. We've roasted all the coffee!" At the time they didn't see the humour in my statement. When the cleaner arrived I said to her, "You are going to need a lot more equipment today!" She too didn't see the humour in the situation.

Realizing that this day was going to be different, I called our key department heads to contact staff and franchisees. At this stage my partner, Nabi Saleh, was still overseas and I wasn't able to get in contact with him until later that morning. My mobile phone began ringing constantly. Every time I turned it off to talk to someone there were ten or more missed calls when it was turned back on. It was impossible to keep up with the phone calls. I soon realized that television interviews (television helicopters were hovering over the warehouse), 31 fire engines, insurance investigators, our own insurance agents, and police and fire investigators were going to take my whole day away. So we conducted hurried meetings with our key people, talked to staff as they arrived, and started to arrange temporary facilities.

While the fire was still raging, I received a phone call to say that two containers had arrived from overseas containing stock that had been in transit. I was asked if I would like the stock delivered to the usual address. After convincing our custom agent that this was not a good idea, we were able to move it into loaned warehouse space. We could then begin to air freight key products to provide ongoing supply.

The fire ended up destroying the warehouse which contained our stock, our roasting equipment, our training facility, and the complete support office for Australia. Fortunately, we still had our green beans and the bulk stock of cups and lids because they were at another location. We had to rent furniture and phone systems just to keep going.

We began storing our equipment and products in my own home and the home of my neighbours, Bob and Jan Gage, to whom I am forever grateful. My partner, Nabi, even had roasted coffee beans stored in his pool cabana. Our legal people worked out of the premises of our legal firm, Coleman and Greig Solicitors, and our internal design team worked out of the offices of Otto Design Interiors, our external design company. Even a friend from our church would not leave until we agreed to use his spare office space for our reception and franchising team. And other business associates loaned us temporary warehouse space.

Your staff are the key to crisis recovery

I attribute our miraculous recovery from this disaster primarily to God. The other key to our recovery was our own people, our franchisees, our friends, our suppliers and business people with whom we had good relationships. We were able to start roasting coffee literally one day after the fire. My partner was able to contact someone he knew who had roasting equipment not being fully utilised. We had our own green beans, and we had our own expert staff who roasted the coffee, so we were quickly able to start supplying our franchisees.

Within 24 hours of the fire starting, we opened two new stores. Because stock for these two stores had already left our premises enroute to the new stores, our delivery hero (who worked day and night during this time), Greg Hillier, asked us if we wanted to postpone the store openings and to re-distribute the stock. At the time I believed it would be a great testimony if we were able to open those stores during the crisis; I felt it would send a strong message that we were still moving forward with a plan, that we were optimistic about the future, and that we were in control of the situation.

Our operational people worked with our franchisees to share stock around. The result was that no store closed during that time. In fact, sales went up! With all the media coverage we were receiving, we had customers coming into our stores saying they were there to support us. (It would have been great if they had waited two or three weeks before giving their support!) In the end, we were able to satisfy everyone and keep producing great cappuccinos and lattes.

I believe it was Henry Ford who once said, "You can take away my cars, you can take away my business, you can take away my money, but leave me my people and we will do it all over again." Through the whole fire episode, Gloria Jean's Coffees certainly bore testimony to that statement. Our team pulled together during this time. They cheerfully worked long hours in less than ideal environments, not just to keep the business going, but to see it actually move a long way forward. And we did move forward from that horrific day! On the day of the fire we even had a potential franchisee call us to say, "I've seen your premises on fire on the news and I'm ringing to enquire about franchising." Now that's what I call optimistic!

From one viewpoint the fire attracted great publicity in Australia and overseas. Television, radio and newspapers covered the whole story with extensive pictures and interviews. The media coverage accelerated our brand awareness. I remarked to Kevin Dorsey, our marketing manager at the time, "You've done a great job in increasing our brand awareness, but please don't do that again!"

The fire was a defining moment in the history of our brand. Our staff stepped up and embraced the challenge. We continued to grow and expand. We ended up moving into larger premises and, looking back, we were soon at a point in which we would not have fitted into the old premises. We grew so quickly after that. And yet, with growth come other challenges.

Some staff need to leave

In his remarkable book Good to Great, Jim Collins talks about the concept of organisations being like a bus. He says that everyone on your team is on a journey on the bus (your organization). Sometimes the bus has to stop, and that's when people get off and new people get on. There are times when some people need to leave your business. Some people may need to grow, and if they no longer fit the growing or changing needs where they are, then they will do better moving on.

When I ran the media department at the large advertising

company I worked for, DDB Needham Advertising, I felt I needed to keep everyone happy and on board the bus. I used to manage staff in order to do exactly that. But I discovered that when someone did leave and a new person joined, the new person brought new passion, new enthusiasm and new ideas that would take us all to a whole new level. I recognized that those who want to leave are obviously not committed to the organisation anymore. When they move to another organisation, in most instances they will grow to a whole new level. But if they had stayed with us, they would have been held back, and in turn the organisation would have been held back. There is a point at which people need to grow, and they will either move and grow within the company, or they will need to expand and move on elsewhere.

So don't be scared to make staff changes. In the early years at Gloria Jean's Coffees we had people covering a variety of jobs. And as we grew we discovered that these jobs became too big and too expansive for those people. We realized that they needed to let go of some tasks, so we brought in new staff. Because people were worried about their jobs, there was resistance to letting go. What they didn't realize was that they were not going to be able to handle the new job, let alone the expanded job they were already working in. There is always a challenge in managing people. Even good people need to learn when to let go and when to delegate and move on.

Hire the right people

One of the mistakes we made in our early years was hiring people we could afford, rather than people who could get the job done. Hiring the wrong people or hiring people you can afford actually does not create a successful future. Whether in accounting, administration or other areas of your business, they can actually create long-term problems for your organisation.

Resumes always look great! You wouldn't expect to be handed a bad resume. So it is crucial to do some background work. For instance, to attempt to get a fair evaluation of a prospective employee, try to find a referee who is not a personal friend or a family member. Then ring them and try to read into the comments they give you.

When interviewing for new staff, ask questions such as:

- What excites you in life?
- How do you view work?
- If pay wasn't an issue, what kind of job would you choose?
- What activities are you involved in outside work?
- What are your dreams for the future?

Present your organisation's vision, mission and values, then ask:

- What is your impression of these?

Whether in retail or in any other type of business, hiring the best of a bad bunch is not a great way to go. If you do not find the right people through the initial interviews, then keep looking. Some franchisees would tell me they had received a lot of enquiries from people wanting to work in their store, but they simply told them there weren't any jobs available. I told them they should never do that because vacancies arise all the time with staff deciding to move on for various reasons. For instance, some staff may leave once they have finished a university course. Others may leave to move interstate or into another industry. You should always be looking for—and collecting details from—potential staff motivated to get a job with you.

Always be on the lookout for good people. If someone gives you great service and impresses you, suggest they give you a call if ever they are looking for a new opportunity. You want those types of people on your team and in your bus. With those types of people—the passionate, caring, enthusiastic ones—you will have fewer stops along the journey.

Another mistake many people make is to only hire people who are less skilled or who have less potential than themselves. These people fear that overqualified staff could either rise to threaten their own position or leave dissatisfied that they could go no further in their job. As a leader in any area of business, you need people who can take you forward, who can do what you cannot do, and who rise to levels of expertise you may never be able to reach. These are the people who, with good management, will not only move you toward your vision, but make you look good, smart and experienced — even in areas you are not good at!

There are probably examples of people in every business who are fearful of hiring experienced, talented staff. This problem even surfaced at Gloria Jean's Coffees. When a department head or franchisee is not secure in their own position, they will only hire people who don't threaten them, don't question their decisions, and don't show any initiative in the way they do their jobs. The culture of their staff is one where all decisions go back to the top, so that the organisation becomes stagnant and uncreative and eventually bogs down. Growth beyond the limitations of the leader becomes impossible.

When this occurs in a store situation, the staff don't take initiative in solving customer issues or in creating sales opportunities. They may not even do the simple things without constant direction. When this happens, the franchisee ends up working far longer hours because he or she cannot rely on inexperienced young staff.

If you are an owner or a department head within a business, be warned that if you have a majority of staff under you with limited potential or skill, this will create enormous problems as you attempt to grow. So watch out for leaders in your business who have this fear of hiring people with more expertise or experience than themselves. The potential exists not only for their departments to stagnate under their leadership, but for your whole business to crumble.

However, there is a balance here. We still need to be training and motivating young, inexperienced staff. We need both kinds of people to help take us forward — those who have done what we aspire to do, as well as those who will learn and grow along the way. What we do not need are leaders who think they can do it all themselves and feel threatened by those they lead.

take action |
NOW!

one: Hire the right people, not necessarily the people you can afford.

two: Look for people with passion, commitment and enthusiasm.

three: Don't be scared to make staff changes.

four: Hire people who are better than yourself and learn to manage them. They will make you look good!

five: If staff leave, recognise that some staff need to leave.

six: Build team spirit by believing in your people and helping them believe in themselves.

seven

BE YOU

Dare to be different, positive, innovative and excellent

"We forfeit three-fourths of ourselves in order to be like other people."
Arthur Schopenhauer, Philosopher

I was one of a number of board directors at DDB Needham Advertising for quite a number of years. One of the board directors was much older than I was and he was responsible for a group of key clients. One day I walked into his office to discuss a client and the first comment he made was, "You know I don't' trust you! I don't trust you because you don't drink and you'll remember everything I say when I've been drinking." He drank constantly and, although he was a direct person when sober, he was even more direct after he'd been drinking. Now, being much younger I could have treated him as a role model and accepted his behaviour, attitudes and lifestyle. But I decided to discount what he was telling me because I didn't want my future linked to him or to his lifestyle.

You also have a choice as to who you adopt as a role model. Make that decision wisely. Your role models will determine your future. You will become like them in language, attitude and behaviour.

I believe you should be constantly looking for people who are positive. Choose people around you who will have a positive input in your life. You need to ignore doubters and negative people. They will only drag you away from your vision.
Some people regard me as being too positive and not accepting of

reality. However, my attitude is that we are constantly bombarded with too many negative influences in life. We desperately need a more positive balance. The media, friends, family and business associates mostly look at life from the bottom of the pile and, while they can point out potential problems in everything, for the most part they don't have any real solutions. Very few people offer positive advice on how you can break through challenges, build your business and be successful.

When the fire had burned our Gloria Jean's Coffees premises to the ground, which included our roasting facility, training facility, warehouse and our whole support structure, many people initially were very supportive and positive. However, about three months after the fire someone commented to my wife, "Do you realise that businesses your size never recover from a fire like that! Within two years they generally go under or the business never reopens. They are never able to recover financially." Well, fortunately I wasn't around to hear that statement at the time. My view back then was, *Well, we have 92 stores open and several more stores opening in the next three months... and all these people need to remain employed. To me it was a question of How do we rebuild ourselves overnight?* Which we did, by the way!

The morning after the fire, I arrived early before any of the other staff turned up. When our key people who roast the coffee and pick orders in the warehouse arrived, they had some very blank faces and looked very discouraged. They felt they'd all lost their jobs and that there was no future at Gloria Jean's Coffees. I said to them, "I don't know where you get that idea from, because we have 92 stores open and we're going to continue to service them. And we're just about to open several more." My partner, Nabi, arrived back from overseas and expressed the same comments to our staff.

As a leader in your company and as a leader in your family, you need to learn to sow life into the people around you. Positive words encourage and build up, and as you express those positive words to your people, they will develop their own vision for their own lives and will want to grow with you. Ignore doubters and negative people; they aren't going to help you. And don't become one of these people yourself, because it will negatively impact those around you.

A positive attitude changes environments

My wife, Sue, remembers an encounter she had with an elderly lady she used to visit regularly. This woman was quite negative at times and would always talk about her problems, and point out the problems with everyone else around her. She had created a whole world of her own in which everyone was against her. Sue refused to accept this attitude and turned every one of this lady's comments into a positive response. During one visit the lady said in exasperation, "It's no use talking to you! I can't complain to you! You won't accept it!"
Sue answered, "You're right."

It wasn't long before their conversations became more positive. Remember that negativity *can* be starved out, and that a positive attitude is attractive and can often change negative environments.

People who haven't experienced any growth or success will find it hard to believe that growth is possible. Those who don't think there's a great future and who only see disasters ahead will give advice influenced by what they believe. When you read a book written by someone who hasn't been successful and who hasn't had any real experience, you need to discount their advice. Someone who has not built a business or conquered tough situations will not be able to provide you with wise advice. That's why not all books, training programs or consultants are going to be useful to you. They do have some advice to offer, but they are limited in what they can provide you.

Sometimes you will need to ignore other people's advice and make your own decisions. In my advertising days, when we were handling a number of supermarket brands, one of the companies was about to launch a new shampoo product. They had prepared for the product launch by the textbook. They had conducted their research and had all their plans lined up. The consumers who were involved in the product research said that they would buy this product based on everything they were told. So the product went onto supermarket shelves, but the company soon realized that the shampoo wasn't selling very well.

When we held a review meeting with the client, I pointed out that they were launching their shampoo alongside dozens of other shampoo products lined up on supermarket shelves. The packaging on their new shampoo looked very similar to other shampoos. When customers looked at the various shampoos to see what they offered, if both the price and the packaging were similar they would not be swayed to choose a shampoo they were not familiar with. What the consumers in the research group had *not* been shown was the new shampoo in comparison to the other shampoos being offered in supermarkets. This tells us that if your research is faulty, your plans are going to be faulty, and your product and business will suffer. Sometimes you need to be prepared to discount textbook research altogether and work to research a product in the context of the real environment. And sometimes that means ignoring what your customers and advisors are telling you.

Learn to be you – don't always follow others

My advice to you is this: Learn to be you; learn to go with your passion and your vision. Yes, listen to people. Yes, read books. But learn to make your own decisions and not allow other people to set your vision. When you allow other people to set your vision, you become a follower and then you become a volunteer.

Conrad Hotels ran an advertisement in magazines which stated: "Be you. Everyone else is taken." Their advertisements were actually promoting hotel rooms, but this is a good slogan for your own life. Learn to be yourself. Don't try to be someone else.

Sometimes the problem with friends or business associates is that they want to turn you or your business into a different business. They would like to see your business moulded into one of their own design. They often observe from afar other businesses that seem successful and they advise you to copy those businesses. They don't understand that those businesses have probably been through difficult times and the directors or owners have had to make a lot of tough decisions to get to where they are today. Friends and associates equally do not realize that your business is uniquely yours. In fact, every business is a reflection of the owner's vision.

Another principle I have learned is that as you grow, develop and build a business, you need to take the high road. By this I mean that you and I should always look to take the innovative road, the road of excellence. People with a large vision find that their road is less congested. On the other hand, it's extremely busy and congested on the low road. Everyone expects to operate there. Everyone competes there. It's the expected route. It's the route that often presents fewer obstacles, although I believe that even on the low road you are going to face obstacles. Whether you take the high road or the low road, you actually cannot avoid problems and difficulties in life.

Benjamin Franklin described insanity as "doing the same thing over and over and expecting different results." That's why you can't follow the low road, because people on the low road keep doing the same things, the same way, whilst expecting a different result.

Learn to do things differently

Learn to grow each year. Learn to stretch and learn to do things differently. Why? Because the world does not stand still and your competitors do not stand still. Your business also will not stand still. Author John Maxwell says he has met people who tell him that they've had ten years experience, and yet he discovers in many instances that they haven't had ten years experience — they've actually had one year's experience ten times. They have been doing the same things the same way for ten years!

At DDB Needham Advertising we were constantly criticized when we were pitching for a new advertising account against other agencies. (This occurred whether they were small, medium or large agencies.) Other agencies would tell prospective clients, the media (who are always looking for stories) or anyone else who would listen that no one was giving their advertising account to DDB Needham Advertising because we were too conservative, we lacked creativity, and we weren't innovative.

Needless to say, while we were being criticized we grew at a fast rate. We grew from a small agency to a medium agency to one of the largest agencies in the country with a client list that was envied by other agencies. We worked hard on excelling. We set our course and we set our vision. We believed in ourselves. We innovated and we produced advertising that worked and produced results. We learned and we grew. We ignored the so-called experts who told us what they thought or perceived who we were. We simply set about being excellent. Eventually we were included on most of the larger potential clients' lists when they were looking to source a new advertising agency.

It's important to note that excellence isn't perfection. Excellence is doing the best you can for every client and for every staff member... excellence in the way you deliver your presentations and in the way you do the job. I want to encourage you to enjoy excelling at everything you do in your business, because when you excel, you enjoy your work, your life, your family and everything else.

Excellence is not an event; it's an attitude. Here are some great statistics from the USA that highlight the value of an attitude of excellence. If you accept 99.9% as good enough, then:

- Two million documents would be lost by the Internal Revenue Service (USA) every year
- 811,000 faulty rolls of 35 millimetre film would be loaded in cameras this year
- 22,000 cheques would be deducted from the wrong bank account in the next 60 minutes
- 12 babies will be given to the wrong parents every day
- Over 268,000 defective tyres will be shipped this year
- 2,488,000 books will be shipped this year with wrong covers
- 3,056 copies of tomorrow's Wall Street Journal will be missing three sections

- 18,300,000 pieces of mail will be mishandled in the next hour
- 291 pacemaker operations will be performed incorrectly this year.

So if you've ever heard the words "that's good enough" or "close enough is good enough" or "well, we've got 99.9 percent", just ask the 291 people who had pacemakers inserted incorrectly whether that's a good enough attitude! So often people will tell you, "Well you got close enough. You don't need to be excellent. You just need to survive." If you operate by this principle, then your whole business will stagnate.

Avoid life-limiting thoughts

Words are powerful because they can either lift you up or push you down. That's why labels tend to stick. When you are young and your parents say, "Oh, she's just a Plain Jane!" or "He'll never be as smart as his brother!" or "You'll never amount to anything!" we tend to drag those life-limiting thoughts around like a ball and chain for the rest of our lives.

Eighty years ago Johnny Weissmuller (also known as Tarzan to moviegoers) was called the greatest swimmer of all time. Doctors and coaches declared, "Nobody will ever break Johnny's records!" He held more than 50 US national swimming titles and set 67 world records. Johnny Weissmuller never lost a race and retired from his amateur swimming career undefeated. Today, 13-year-old girls break Johnny Weissmuller's records on a regular basis!

For decades experts stated that nobody would break the four-minute-mile barrier, but Roger Bannister refused to believe it. As a result, he broke the so-called 'impossible' four-minute-mile. Today, hundreds of runners break it every year. Personally, I haven't broken that record....yet!

Understand this: Others can stop you temporarily, but you are the only one who can do it permanently. How do you overcome life-limiting thoughts and negative labels? American poet Edgar Guest wrote:

There are thousands to tell you it cannot be done,
There are thousands to prophesy failure;
There are thousands to point out to you, one by one,
The dangers that wait to assail you.
But just buckle in with a bit of a grin,
Just take off your coat and go to it;
Just start to sing as you tackle the thing
That 'cannot be done', and you'll do it.

To succeed at any worthwhile venture you need a thick skin, especially when it comes to handling criticism. That's what separates those who say they want something from those who say they are prepared to pay the price to get it. For example, if you want an increase in your business, are you giving outstanding service to your current clients? Remember, a peacock that rests on its feathers is just another turkey.

Sometimes we are in love with the image of success, but we haven't counted the actual cost of succeeding. Often we want everything now — especially when we start a business, because that's what we believe we should have. But if we get it now, it will probably destroy us because we may not be equipped to handle it yet.

I always felt that when we started Gloria Jean's Coffees it would be good to open with 100 stores, but we didn't have the infrastructure for that size. We simply weren't ready to handle that number of franchisees, that number of sales, and everything else that goes with that level of success. We needed to work our way through the growth stages and build our structure and our team. Today we have over 400 stores. That number of stores would not have been possible in the early years. We needed to learn. We needed to grow. We needed to overcome the 'can't be done' thinking and put into place people and processes to be able to support that level of success.

take action | NOW!

one: Practice being positive to people. Start by giving at least one unsolicited comment of praise to someone each day.

two: After each day concludes, ask yourself, *What situations should I have been positive in?*

three: Learn to continually stretch yourself and learn to do things differently..

four: Apply a spirit of excellence to everything you do.

five: Shake off life-limiting thoughts and negative labels that hold you back from your real potential.

six: Notice and be inspired by the *remarkable* around you. Ask yourself, *What remarkable things did I experience this week? What remarkable comments did I hear this week? What remarkable decisions did I take part in this week?* Then ask yourself, *How could these apply to my business?*

seven: Find some thinking time. Choose one area of your business each week and think through creative ways to improve that area. Approach it from all viewpoints, with no restrictions, and with a sense of fun. Have your staff come up with ideas as well.

eight |

MARKETING

"When the product is right, you don't have to be a great marketer."
Lee Iacocca

Marketing is crucial to your business success. So many of us are wasting our money and efforts in marketing strategies that just don't work. Most businesses have a 'hit-and-miss' approach to marketing. Why? Because that's what our competitors are doing! They don't know any different and they're just following the crowd. But marketing is all about being different - standing out in the crowd. And the reason most of us aren't doing that is because we don't understand marketing and what it can achieve for us.

In my 30 years in the advertising and marketing industry (with a heavy emphasis on advertising), I have discussed advertising and marketing strategies with thousands of individuals who have worked in a variety of marketing companies, advertising agencies, and associated support companies. I discovered at some stage through my career that most people believe advertising is marketing. News flash: It actually isn't! Advertising is only part of the total marketing picture.

During my three decades in advertising I noticed a number of companies that had an employee designated to 'Sales and Marketing', but these employees were actually managing the sales force and viewed all dollars spent as related to the sales force. The result was that very little funding was spent on other elements of marketing, and this affected the overall success and profitability of the business. In other companies I noticed an employee in charge of marketing, another employee in charge of the sales force, and an office manager responsible for the design and purchase of stationery. In effect, these companies weren't portraying one clear message because they had divided up marketing into a few different departments that didn't talk to each other. These different departments were each producing materials that didn't communicate a clear, consistent message to their customers.

The role of advertising within marketing

Marketing really involves a wide range of areas. Not all of them are relevant to every business. The more common elements of marketing include: public relations, pricing, signage, location, website, packaging, stationery, telemarketing, advertising and receptionist. Note that this is not a complete list. For instance, it doesn't include word-of-mouth, visual communication and written communication. But it does provide an overall view.

MARKETING PIE

Here is a pie chart that shows marketing's true role in business. In the centre of the pie chart you will notice the words 'core idea'. We developed this particular idea in our advertising days because we needed to come up with a 'core idea' for a product or service which was then communicated through all these elements. This helped us to speak with one voice whenever the company was communicating a message. This was very efficient for us because, no matter what size advertising budget our client had — whether $500 or $50,000 or $5 million or $50 million — we would find that the same message was actually building that brand or service and we didn't have conflicting messages fighting with each other.

This is a very effective way to build your brand. The same message or core idea is consistently being communicated to your different target audiences. It may be executed in different ways to your various target audiences, but overall the marketplace is receiving the same message.

The core idea of MacTime

Let me give you some examples of an effective use of this strategy. The advertising agency I worked with in the 1990s developed the core idea of 'MacTime' for McDonald's. This concept came out of planning and review sessions with the various franchisees in each state. The MacTime idea in itself did not come out of these meetings, but discussions with those who had direct customer contact generated the idea amongst our creative people.

Once the core idea of MacTime was established, any message from then on that promoted breakfast, lunch or dinner always centered around MacTime. This was true, whether it was to older people or to young families, whether it was in Bathurst or Ballarat, and whether it was communicated through public relations or advertising. For any individual, at any time of day and in any situation in life, MacTime meant McDonald's. When people were on the road and needed to stop for a quick snack, if it was breakfast time, then it was MacTime. Likewise, if it was a toilet break during a car trip, then it was MacTime. If it was dinner time, then it was MacTime. If the kids were restless and needed a break (in a fun playground), it was MacTime. If you were driving in the country and encouraged by the Roads and Traffic Authority's "Stop. Revive. Survive." road signs, then McDonald's provided for that situation with clean toilets, a reasonably priced restaurant and consistent food. Anyone could sit and relax in a McDonald's restaurant for a few minutes, at any time.

We knew we had achieved the results we wanted from this message when we saw it implemented in the community. The media began using the word 'MacTime' in stories related to McDonald's. On one occasion I was following two police cars along a road when I noticed the first car displaying the word 'MacTime' followed by '⇦' on the digital readout sign on top of its roof. The lead police car then indicated to turn left and drove into a McDonald's restaurant car park, immediately followed by the second police car. The officers in the second police car understood the simple message that was being displayed on the first car's rooftop sign. Another example of the simplicity and widespread embrace of the MacTime message was when a number of road signs began cropping up on country roads with the large McDonald's golden arches "M" logo followed by the words "time – 2km" - indicating the distance in kilometers to the next McDonald's restaurant. Travellers knew that it was MacTime—whatever time of day— and that MacTime was only 2km away.

The core idea of Roses Only

Another example of a business that has used a simple, consistent core idea in all its marketing is Roses Only. Roses Only began using this concept in the 1990s. The Roses Only concept was that you could ring an 1800 phone number and a dozen roses would be ordered, delivered and charged to your credit card. Roses Only paid for small newspaper advertisements placed strategically in the sports and business pages of daily newspapers. These small advertisements displayed one very simple message: 'Roses Only. Roses by the dozen. Phone 1300 ROSESONLY' You may ask, "Why place advertisements in the sports and business pages and not up the front of the newspaper?" Because the campaign was obviously targeted to men, and men tend to read those two sections. The advertisements prompted men to remember an anniversary, a birthday, the need to say sorry… It was a simple call to action. Roses Only said one thing, and that was the message portrayed in everything the business did. That was their core idea.

The core idea of Gloria Jean's Coffees

Some years after we launched Gloria Jean's Coffees into the Australian market, we carried out some research which showed us that our customers saw Gloria Jean's Coffees as a place for a short break. The car may have broken down, the kids were playing up, mum and dad were facing financial issues, there may have been strife at work… and customers told us through this research that they saw Gloria Jean's Coffees as an oasis or a respite from their hectic schedule. Their break was that few minutes having a nice cup of coffee. They could relax in a Gloria Jean's Coffees store. Even if they didn't stay in the store, they could grab their cup of coffee and keep going, taking with them that relief from the busyness of the day.

Our advertising agency came up with the line "Escape the Daily Grind". Yes, it was a play on the coffee term 'grind', but it was the actual grind of life that people were experiencing… and they needed a break from it. They saw Gloria Jean's Coffees not as something to fix their problems forever, but as a short break where they could escape from it all. We worked hard at putting that theme into everything, from advertisements and brochures to napkins and cups.

Becoming remarkable

Another aspect of marketing is the industry catch-cry: 'Become remarkable'. In the book *Purple Cow*, author Seth Godin talks about companies needing to become remarkable with their product or service. He says that so many companies are saying the same thing, providing the same service, and no one is standing out. He tells the story of driving down a freeway in Europe with his family when they notice a brown-spotted cow. With excitement everyone says, "Look, a brown-spotted cow!" The same thing happens when they see the next brown-spotted cow. But after a couple of kilometres brown-spotted cows became boring and commonplace. So Seth thought to himself, *What if we suddenly saw a purple-spotted cow? Now that would be different! That would stand out! That would be remarkable!*

That is what we need to do with our businesses: stand out! I have a friend who joined a real estate company recently as part of their sales team. This is an industry that talks about service, but generally people in real estate all offer the same service and charge the same fees. This company came up with the '1%' core idea: Their real estate business would undertake all transactions on a one percent commission. The company was criticized by its industry. The staff received abusive phone calls and letters. All types of rude remarks were aimed at them. My friend was told that this concept would not work and that the real estate company he worked for would not survive. But he and his team worked on the basis of 'being first' and 'standing out'. As a result, their business has grown substantially and they are generating an enormous amount of listings and sales. I can guarantee you that within the next few years many other real estate agents will be copying the '1%' commission concept rather than coming up with innovative and remarkable ideas of their own.

I experienced the same situation when I worked in advertising. One of my clients insisted on advertising in certain trade publications. He decided that that was where his competitors advertised and therefore that should be the right place to advertise. I later met with other advertising agency personnel who were buying for their clients in these same trade magazines and I asked the question, "Why do you advertise in those trade publications?" Almost every one of them replied, "We advertise there because your client advertises there!" Amazingly, no one was advertising in those trade publications simply because it was the right place to advertise; they were doing it because their competitors were doing it!

Do something different

If the consumer believes salt is salt, sugar is sugar, and coffee is coffee — and price is the determining factor — then at Gloria Jean's Coffees we needed to convince the consumer of the quality of our coffee and the difference of our total coffee experience. In every brand you need to create a difference. You need to stand out. You need to become remarkable. In your own business category, you need to find out what everybody else is doing and then do something different.

Some of the businesses that have become remarkable over the years include Dell, Wal-Mart, Southwest Airlines and Gloria Jean's Coffees. Charlie Bell, former President and CEO of McDonald's Corporation, said, "Everything we do influences our brand image—the stores, the service, the advertising, the uniforms, the cleanliness of our playgrounds, the seats, décor, the quality of the toys used in the promotions—everything." A lot of businesses think that branding is just advertising. They are wrong! Branding is *everything* you do.

Other companies I have worked with recently are becoming remarkable in their industries. Australian Opal Cutters supplies jewellery, such as opals and pearls. The owners conduct their business from the third level of a building in the city CBD, rather than at the retail level. This allows them to avoid paying exorbitant city CBD rents. They are able to offer 50 to 55 percent off the normal retail price of any of their jewellery products. And they provide outstanding customer service. They have become remarkable in the way they do their business, despite their competitors in the industry all using the same old traditional tactics to try to gain dominance. Their competitors may criticize them, but they are themselves continually fighting each other to stay ahead, to stay in business.

Another example of a remarkable new company is Save on Bills. Rather than deal in just one area of savings for customers, this company is able to provide a complete package for clients. It helps businesses and individuals to save money by looking at the best deals in a variety of services, including insurance, financing, telecommunications, water and electricity, credit cards and internet service provision. Save on Bills reviews what customers are paying and provides a better service at a substantially reduced price. This adds more money to the customer's pocket. Save on Bills stands out because no one else offers this comprehensive service across such a range of products.

Gloria Jean's Coffees is remarkable

When Gloria Jean's Coffees started in Australia, we were told that it would not work. We were told that people would not accept the take-away cup. We were told that people want table service and cooked meals. In the end, they were probably right. These statements were delivered from past and current experience, and as such they were statements of small, limited thinking. Unintentionally, through the introduction of the brand, we were able to turn the coffee industry on its ear.

Today Gloria Jean's Coffees operates at an incredible level in terms of volume — way above what it was when we started. The whole Australian mindset of drinking coffee and tea outside the home has changed. The way we meet and catch up with each other has changed. We now live in a 'meet for a coffee' lifestyle. It is now normal to conduct a business meeting or an interview at a Gloria Jean's Coffees store. Where once Australians would normally have a coffee in a china cup while sitting with a meal, today we are more likely to grab a coffee on the run. This is happening not only in the 20- to 40-year age group, it is also true for teenagers, young families and senior citizens. Gloria Jean's Coffees became remarkable by developing a marketing strategy, having a vision, being focused, saying the same thing (speaking with one voice), breaking the pattern, and then expecting (and measuring) results.

Al Capone was once asked, "Why do you keep robbing banks?" "That is where the money is," he replied.

Like Al Capone, my advice to you is: Aim to target people "where the money is". It's fine simply selecting a target audience, but if they are not interested in your product or service then you are not going to be successful.

The tipping point

I recently read an interesting book by Malcolm Gladwell called *The Tipping Point*. Although in some places the book is slow going, one of the great stories in the book is about Hush Puppies, a well-known shoe company in the USA. In 1994 the company was down to about 30,000 pairs of Hush Puppies in America. For a marketing and manufacturing company, these were very poor sales figures in a country of that size. At a fashion shoot one day, two Hush Puppies executives met a stylist from New York. The stylist had heard that Hush Puppies were experiencing a small resurgence in New York as they were becoming hip in Manhattan nightclubs and bars. In 1995 Hush Puppies sold 430,000 pairs of shoes, up from 30,000 in the previous year. The next year saw four times that amount sold. Hush Puppies had not done anything differently, but they discovered that young non-conformists were buying their brand of shoes in small shops in the Bronx because the shoes were *not* the 'in thing' at that time. They were buying Hush Puppies to look different and they were wearing them to the discos and bars. Others who saw these young people wearing the unusual shoes decided to copy these kids because they saw them as the 'in thing'. Sales of Hush Puppies started to escalate. In the end, sales of Hush Puppies soared to four million per year. Naturally the non-conformist younger market soon deserted Hush Puppies after they were no longer an alternative product.

As I look back at when Gloria Jean's Coffees started in Australia, in 1996 we hadn't read the book *The Tipping Point*. In fact, it wasn't published until 2000. The 'tipping point' concept certainly wasn't on our agenda or in our thought processes. But as I review the last ten years of Gloria Jean's Coffees, I realize that as we came into the market, we actually attracted that small group of people that embraced the concept (called 'early adopters') of quality coffee, flavoured coffee, and convenient coffee prepared in the way they liked. These people launched Gloria Jean's Coffees into the marketplace through 'word of mouth' and through stories that appeared in the media. We tipped over the edge into the mass market, something the coffee and tea industry in Australia had never before achieved.

You too can do the same thing with your product or service. But you need to be brave. You need to be bold. You need to stand out. And you need to do something different. If your marketing staff, marketing agency or marketing consultant is not innovative or does not have a 'becoming remarkable' attitude, then challenge them to do so or find someone who does.

take action | NOW!

Simple marketing clues

Here are some simple clues on marketing that you may be able to implement in your own business:

one: **Strategy**. Develop a strategy for your brand or service and then everyone in the company needs to buy into that strategy.

two: **Focus**. You need to have a single-minded focus on what your marketing needs to achieve for your business. Don't be distracted by what your competitors are doing or by clever marketing gimmicks. Stick to your strategy.

three: **Speak with one voice**. You cannot say or promise too many things or you will confuse people. All your marketing tools — whether your brochure or your website or newspaper advertisements — need to speak with one voice and one message.

four: **Don't try to communicate everything.** Too many companies want to include the full book about their product or service in a magazine advertisement or television commercial. All they successfully do is bore everyone and turn customers off.

five: **Break the pattern.** Whatever you are doing now, you are not standing out. You may feel comfortable and happy because you are employing nice, traditional communication tactics. But you need to break the pattern and be uncomfortable with it. Then you will stand out and see results.

six: **Reflect who you want to be**. Make sure your advertising and everything you do in marketing is a reflection of what you want to portray as a company. What do you stand for as a company? Does everything you do — spoken, written and visual (such as colours and typeface) — reflect your company or product?

seven: **How do you measure success?** If you are a retailer and your product is sold through supermarkets, you expect cash registers to ring. If you are in the service industry, you need sales leads. If you are trying to change the image of your company, you need to have some trigger in place that enables you to measure whether your marketing is working. Good marketing is extremely powerful, so just spending money on marketing and not measuring the results is poor management.

eight: **The timing of your success.** You need to know *what* you want your marketing to achieve... and by *when*? A timeline is important. It also needs to be realistic and achievable.

nine: **Research.** Research can be a great tool in marketing, but it can also be overused and abused. Make sure your business is creating statistics, not just measuring them. I have often sat with clients to watch research companies conduct surveys and focus groups. I have then skimmed across the research data provided after the event and come to my own conclusions about where we need to go. It's fine if researchers provide their own overview for you, but in the end they often do not understand your product or service... or even your market. Most of their work is done in a clinical environment and it can only give you a view based on that research.

The co-founder of advertising firm Doyle Dane Bernbach International, Bill Bernbach, once said, "We are so busy measuring public opinion that we forget we can mold it. We are so busy listening to statistics we forget we can create them." This is a very succinct statement regarding research and extremely important to take note of. We need to realize that we can actually go out and create the market! We can go out and build the market to a new level. And we don't need research to help us do that. Research has a role, however often research will only hold us back.

nine

KEEP LEARNING

Gain wisdom from every experience

"Many people dream of success. To me, success can only be achieved through repeated failure and introspection."
Soichiro Honda, founder of Honda Motors

When Nabi and I began the Gloria Jean's Coffees journey in 1996, we soon realized how little retail experience we actually had! There were many things we had never done before, such as the process of acquiring suitable sites and negotiating rents, as well as finding store designers and shop fitters. These aspects of retailing were new to both of us. We decided we needed some help and we needed to learn quickly.

We made initial contact with the head of leasing at Westfield in Australia (one of the world's largest shopping centre groups) at that time, Gary Pinter, who offered us sites at Sydney's Miranda and Eastgardens shopping malls (in Sydney) for our first stores. He gave us help and advice which, on reflection, was invaluable. It would have been easy for us to play the 'negotiation game' and not listen to him or believe what he said. However, we recognised that this man was genuine in wanting our business to succeed, so we remained open to his input.

We came to realize that there are a multitude of areas that need to be covered in a franchising business, and that no one can know it all. So we listened to the advice of many people, including those who worked with transport companies. They gave us advice on how best to ship goods around the country. We learned (sometimes the hard way) that products like chocolate-coated coffee beans do not survive container transport across the Nullarbor Desert in Australia!

Not only did we need to learn *from* these people, sometimes we needed to learn *with* them. We learned alongside a variety of companies that supplied our ingredients, paper goods, retail products and equipment. One of those companies was Kerry Foods, a company that has worked hard with us over a long period. Together, both Gloria Jean's Coffees and Kerry Foods have learned and grown successfully. They have always been open to developing new recipes together with new labeling and packaging. We have also learned from — and been open to — their expertise in the food ingredient area. Both companies benefit when people are open in this way.

So always be willing to learn from any situation. If you don't continue to learn, you won't continue to grow. And if *you* don't grow, neither will your business. Commit to continually look around you for opportunities to invest in your skills and your attitude or mindset.

The process of learning begins now. If you are considering launching a new business, then your education starts now. Here are some tips that are crucial to the success of your new business. First, don't underestimate the costs of starting a business. I have always been told that when you prepare your profit and loss when starting a business, in the first year you should halve the profit in your plan and then halve it again. Then you will probably be close to being right. This may not be an exact formula, however there are so many set-up and ongoing costs which often aren't anticipated. Expected sales levels are often not achieved in the early days. And all of this affects your anticipated business plan.

My second tip is this: If you are starting a business, the first year is spent establishing your foundations as a business. There is a cost to do that and you need to work out how you will get through that year financially. Someone once wisely said, "If you fail to plan, you plan to fail."

I recently worked with an associate who had some major difficulties in his business. He ended up in legal battles and is now facing liquidation. However, he doesn't want to deal with these issues. Somehow he seems to think they will go away and he's always talking about the next venture. Now, that's not such a bad thing; it means he is looking ahead to the future. But he has to still deal with the current financial and legal issues, otherwise they will become anchors around his neck that potentially could drag him down and finally sink him. He needs to take a few steps backwards to deal with these matters and then move forward. My advice to him is that he can learn from this experience… and he can learn from those around him who are available to offer guidance.

Use every opportunity to learn

If you are serious about being successful in business, then always remain open to learn from others around you. I don't just mean learning from friends and colleagues. For instance, I believe you should never leave any conference without first learning at least one thing that will affect your daily life or your business. The same goes for tapes, CDs and books; never finish one without being challenged to improve your life or business. In many cases you will come away with a number of issues that you can address. It's not just a matter of writing these down and reading them. You need to start *applying* these lessons in your business and in your life. Ask yourself this question: *How will I apply this idea?* Then actively do it.

Use your car as a university. Rather than listening to the radio all the time, get your hands on some stimulating leadership or motivational teaching CDs and play them in your car as you drive. If you are weak in the area of customer service, then get some CDs on customer service. If you are weak on relationships, then find CDs offering valuable advice on relationships and listen to those. There are many great resources available all around us.

If you attend seminars or conventions and you hear some great speakers, buy their messages on CD. Check out bookstores for business leadership publications, especially those written by people who have achieved success. Continue to learn and listen to what other people have done. Talk to people who have already reached where you want to go. Allow them to show you how to get there. I find I learn from those with a bit of humour, and even topics that seem unrelated to business help to grow my awareness and relationships. Many of us think we can't learn anything after a certain age. The fact is that we will all be learning until the day we die!

Cultivate curiosity

Twice a year, Pastor Phil Baker from Riverview Church in Perth (Australia) runs 'Building Business Leaders' breakfasts in Australia's capital cities. One of the principles he presents from the life of Leonardo da Vinci is this: Cultivate your curiosity. Curiosity may have killed the cat, but it certainly adds zest to your life. Curiosity helps you grow and develop. It expands your knowledge and your interests. And it spices up your friendships.

Albert Einstein said: "The important thing is not to stop questioning. Curiosity has its own reason for existing. One cannot help but be in awe when he contemplates the mysteries of eternity, of life, of the marvellous structure of reality."

Here are some tips to help you make the most of curiosity:
1. Curiosity is not just about asking questions, it's also about the quality of your questions. When you meet people, develop the ability to ask the *right* questions.
2. Take notes. This helps you record your thoughts and your progress. It helps you document your ideas.
3. Look up the things that challenge you or the creative ideas that are of interest to you. Delve into your curiosity and explore concepts and ideas. Curiosity unfulfilled will quickly dull your life.

Don't become stifled into a box or set parameters that you can't break through. Part of continually learning is that we remain flexible and open to possibilities. So often we set up walls into which our business fits snugly. We live in a world that is growing and expanding at an increasingly fast pace, so as our businesses grow, we also need to learn to expand. We need to learn how to put into place flexible structures so that our businesses don't become boxed in. If we don't, then our rigid structures may restrict us from embracing opportunities to expand.

Embracing a learning attitude means that you are less likely to stay where you are. You will want to be able to look back a year from now and see some great growth in yourself and in your business. A mindset of continual learning will stimulate momentum. A long time ago, US humorist and showman Will Rogers said, "Even if you are on the right track, you'll get run over if you just sit there." Your business could be very successful right now, but without an attitude of learning that leads to forward momentum, your business could slow down a year from now. Just being on the right track won't help your business if you lose momentum.

Don't wait for success

Continue to learn and grow. The legendary UCLA basketball coach John Wooden once stated, "When opportunity comes, it's too late to prepare." Learn now. Prepare now for the moment when opportunity arrives. Don't sit around waiting for investors to come or customers to call or a major client to knock on your door. As the old saying goes, "The harder I work, the luckier I get!" Oprah Winfrey once stated, "Luck is a matter of preparation meeting opportunity."

Learn to regularly take stock of your situation. Continue to question where you are and where you are going. Dr Lawrence C. Helms said, "Successful people make the most out of where they are in life today." So where are you today? What is it that you have in your hands? What opportunities do you have before you right now that you may not be fully utilising?

I have found that it is always easier to stay comfortable where you are. It's more challenging to innovate, think ahead and learn new ways to do things. As we were growing Gloria Jean's Coffees through store openings across the country, we believed in the specialty coffee concept and in our product offering. We constantly challenged ourselves to remain open to ideas so that the business could grow to a greater level. We reviewed our cold coffee and tea drink range and our merchandise and food offering on a regular basis (and we still do). With the introduction of new products, we have been able to grow store sales and the average customer dollar transaction.

Before the invention of the spin-dry washing machine in the early 1950s, after washing their clothes people would wring out as much water as possible so their clothes would dry quicker on the line. There's a lesson in that for us: Growing in character and maturity calls for more than just letting life happen; it calls for wringing the wisdom out of every experience. How do you do that? By asking yourself, *What can I learn here? Could I have done this differently?*

Great chess players win because they think several moves ahead. Wisdom asks, "Where does this lead? What are the possible unintended consequences of my decision?" Wise people realise that what they do today will affect tomorrow. Successful business people are always thinking ahead, and they are always learning and preparing. In the Book of Proverbs we are encouraged to pursue wisdom: "Tune your ears to the world of Wisdom; set your heart on a life of Understanding." (Proverbs 2:3-5)

Value a learning attitude

Unfortunately too many people have stopped learning and never grow. Too many people can't break out of their comfort zones. Too many people think to themselves, *I know everything!* You may have heard the saying, "Employ a teenager while they still know everything." No matter what age you are right now, hold on to a learning attitude.

Do you know that *TV Guide* magazine in the USA is the most recognizable and bestselling magazine of its kind in that country? What are Americans learning?! Did you also know that 50 percent of all college students in the USA stop reading after graduation, even though a degree can become outdated in as little as five years?

That's not a new problem in the twenty-first century. Even in the Old Testament, God told the writer of the Book of Hosea, "My people are destroyed for lack of knowledge." Over and over in the Book of Proverbs we are encouraged to gain wisdom:

> Happy *is* the man *who* finds wisdom,
> And the man *who* gains understanding;
> For her proceeds *are* better than the profits of silver,
> And her gain than fine gold.
> She *is* more precious than rubies,
> And all the things you may desire cannot compare with her.
> (Proverbs 3:13-15)

Knowledge is important. It doesn't stop when you graduate from college or when you leave a seminar. Knowledge is part of our journey. It's a part of learning. And whilst knowledge is valuable, *applying* knowledge is just as crucial. Reading books or listening to CD messages alone are not much value if we don't apply what we have learned. What you are learning today through the pages of this book will help you if you put these principles into practice.

take action | NOW!

one: Buy a notebook or journal and take it to all future events you will be attending and where someone will be speaking.

two: Keep a notebook near your television set so that you can write down anything that challenges you while you watch television.

three: Buy CDs or books on topics in which you believe you need input right now (and actually listen to or read them).

four: Ask questions of successful people you know; learn both from their accomplishments and from their mistakes.

five: Cultivate your curiosity; it helps you grow and develop.

ten

FINISHING STRONG

Running stumble-free doesn't make you a winner,
finishing strong does!

"He conquers who endures."
Persius

Australian author and motivational speaker Catherine De Vyre
once stated, "If you can find a path with no obstacles, it probably
leads nowhere." There are so many things that can knock us
down, like cashflow, people, fire, health, unity... Even the little
things, like gossip and rumours, have the potential to derail our
plans. It is no use having a great vision and plan, but not making
any progress because of obstacles or difficulties.

We can learn a lot from that blow-up rubber toy with the weight
at the bottom. When you hit it, it falls over, but it bounces right
back up again. Like that blow-up children's toy, we have to learn
to not stay down. If we stay down, we may never be able to get
up again. If we stay knocked down, we will have lost, because
that is the signal that we are finished, that we are defeated. Poet
H. Lena Jones once wrote, "You're never down, you're either up
or in the process of getting up." Every time we get hit, we have to
learn to get back up and face the challenge in front of us. Scottish
spiritual guru Eileen Caddy once said:

> *The secret of making something work in your lives, is, first of all, the
> deep desire to make it work. Then the faith and belief that it can work.
> Then to hold that clear definite vision in your consciousness and see it
> working out step by step, without one thought of doubt or disbelief.*

The issues we faced at Gloria Jean's Coffees in the early days prepared us for the bigger issues we face today. If we hadn't faced the smaller challenges (although they were large for our size at that stage in the company's growth), we would not be able to face the challenges that confront us today. So face your challenges today. Don't run away or stay knocked down because these obstacles are going to strengthen you to continue your journey. If you overcome today's challenges, you'll be better equipped to face tomorrow's challenges.

We have to admit that we sometimes cause our own stumbling blocks. Look at some of the following issues and see if any of these are limiting your progress and your success:

1. Pride
2. Competitiveness
3. An unforgiving spirit (Don't allow bitterness to get inside your spirit because these are the things that will create unforgiveness.)
4. Immaturity
5. Selfishness (Self-centredness).

If you want the ability to easily overcome obstacles, if you want to finish strongly, then deal with these issues. Each one can hold you back from your true potential. If you want to build your career or your business, then deal now with these issues in your life. Your effectiveness will be limited if these issues remain a part of your character.

In life there are three kinds of people:

1. Those who start wrong, but finish right
2. Those who start right, but finish wrong
3. Those who are afraid to start.

Only one of these kinds of people arrives at the finish line. The good news for many of us is that we can start wrong and still finish strongly. We can stumble at the start and fall over along the way, but we can all finish strongly.

At DDB Needham Advertising we went through a time where we lost five clients in a two-month period. This created a negative impact, further accelerated by the reaction of other advertising agencies, advertising media journalists, and even our own staff. We needed to quickly re-group, make sure our staff were re-focused, stabilize existing clients, and build stability to start to grow again.

At Gloria Jean's Coffees there have been many instances of people starting out with great plans and then hitting unforeseen stumbling blocks. Some work through these to finish strongly, while others struggle. I remember one young couple began their franchise with great plans and dreams. They both worked hard and their store flourished. However, for a variety of reasons their relationship began to deteriorate and, for a time, they separated. Unwilling to see the end of their dreams, they both decided to make a fresh start, change the way they worked and related together, and see their plans go forward. Today they are happily married with a growing family and they run several successful stores. The path was not easy, but they are finishing strong.

Don't be afraid to try

The following anonymous poem describes the third kind of person:

> *There was a very cautious man,*
> *who never laughed or cried.*
> *He never risked, he never lost,*
> *he never won nor tried.*
> *And when he one day passed away,*
> *his insurance was denied,*
> *For since he never really lived,*
> *they claimed he never died.*

Which one of the three are you? Remember: It's not too late to change.

Our fears can be based on the worst lies in the world. Our fears will try to convince us of many things that aren't true. For this reason, we should never make decisions based on our fears. Instead we should:

1. *Tackle fear head on*

As a child, best-selling author Bill Hybels was very timid, but his father kept challenging him. Hybels says his father would take him down to the produce company his father ran and bark out, "Billy, back in that semi!"

Hybels says he dragged himself into the cab of that 40-foot rig shaking with fear. "Sometimes it would take me 45 minutes (to reverse the semi-trailer) and the truck would be half jackknifed, but when I called out, Dad would say, 'Good job!' And the next time it would be easier." So how do you conquer your fear? By confronting it head on.

One of the greatest fears people face is the fear of public speaking, whether addressing staff or doing a more formal presentation. In my early days both at the advertising agency and as a youth leader in my church, I constantly found myself having to speak in front of groups. I gradually developed confidence and learned to improve by watching the good and bad habits of other presenters. I found the way to beat fear in this area was just to do it anyway.

2. *Hang out with courageous people*

King Solomon said, "He who walks with the wise grows wise." (Proverbs 13:20) Success rubs off, but so does failure. Don't hang around with people who habitually cave in or play it safe. Hang out with courageous people. If you can't find any, then be encouraged to stay firm and keep looking out for them. Look for people who encourage you to go for it, people who build you up.

3. *Go for it*

Courage isn't optional—it's foundational. You need it to live each day. You need it to build a better relationship with your business partner and with your spouse. You need it to expand your business and to tackle your bad habits.

4. *Believe you can make it*

Have you heard the story about the old farmer whose mule fell into a well? Since there was no way to get him out, the farmer decided to bury him there. But the mule had a different idea. Initially, when the shovels of dirt began landing on him, he became hysterical. Then this thought struck him: *Just shake it off and step on it!* So he did. Hour after hour as the dirt fell on him he kept telling himself, *Just shake it off and step on it!* No matter how much dirt they threw on him, he just kept shaking it off and stepping on it, until finally he stepped triumphantly out of the well. Life will either bless you or bury you. The difference lies in having the right attitude. When they throw dirt on you, just shake it off and step on it. Or use it as fertilizer and grow stronger!

No one can make you inferior without your consent. What's important is not what others say about you, it's what you say to yourself after they get through talking. When the criticism stops, how do you react? Do you believe them or do you shake off their words? When you decide to *seize the moment* and move ahead, you will often leave others behind, like friends and family… and some of them won't be too happy about that. The only way to avoid experiencing any kind of opposition is to do nothing and stay where you are, and that's simply not acceptable.

When I was heading up the media department of DDB Needham Advertising, one day we decided to take a stand and not buy any advertising time on a particular television network. The reason for this decision was that we had received bad treatment from this station the previous year. Our advertising account was a significant one and the advertising representative from this television network was not happy. Rather than commit to improving his service and rates (not just mouth the usual promises), he decided to try maligning my character. He promised I would never again work in the advertising industry, that my name would be mud, and he would see to it that my reputation was destroyed. While the vindictiveness of the phone call shocked and initially upset me, I knew there was nothing he could do. I knew that there was no 'dirt' he could dig up and all his efforts would probably only serve to show his own character for what it was. Needless to say, the whole threat blew over. Sometimes all you need to do when under threat is stand firm and not overreact or respond in kind.

In the sci-fi series *Babylon 5*, G'Kar asked Garabaldi—the man in charge of station security—to do something difficult. Garabaldi replied, "It could be hard and difficult."
G'Kar answered, "Anything worthwhile will be hard."

When I talk to franchisees and they say to me, "This is really hard work!" I reply, "Well, if it was easy, everyone would be doing it!"

Focus on endurance, not speed

Seasoned long-distance runners have learned to focus on endurance over speed. They pace themselves so that as they approach the finish line they can pull out all stops. There will be disappointments, delays and obstacles that can knock you down along the way, but don't be satisfied with just sitting on the sideline cheering for those who have paid the price to run the race. You will only endure the pain when you have something to look forward to. Crossing the finish line will bring you that reward, whether it's a trophy, money, applause, sponsorship or just a fit and healthy body.

In my earlier chapter on vision, I said that having a vision will keep you focused and on track. Success comes only when you are committed and have the passion to cross the finish line. Set your eye on the goal, run to win, and you're sure to cross the finish line!

In November 1986 Bob Wieland crossed the finish line as New York City Marathon's 19,413th and final finisher. At 40 years of age he was the first person to complete a marathon running with his arms. He'd had his legs blown off in Vietnam and had learned to get around using his arms. He recorded the slowest time in the marathon's history, but at the end of the race he said this: "Success is not based on where you start. It's where you finish and I finished!" With two good legs and all our faculties intact, most of us won't even get out of bed an hour earlier to discover and pursue our God-given destiny!

If you think you've got difficulties to overcome, David Jurd should put you to shame. David Jurd was Director of Operations for Abigroup in Australia when Abigroup was commissioned with the construction of the M7 Westlink Freeway in Sydney. The M7 was to link with the M4 Western Motorway. In an article published in *BRW Magazine* (April 12, 2007) Jurd described the challenge he faced:

The sheer size of the planned road was daunting. These are big tenders with big risks and I can clearly remember reviewing this tender and thinking the biggest risk was getting all that stuff done in the timeframe. I would have said that building it on time was difficult and building it a few months early was getting towards impossible. To turn around and deliver it eight months early - well it reinforces to me that anything is possible.

Jurd said there were three factors that made the project unique in road construction:
1 The number of bridges
2. The consortium and having to build a factory from scratch to assemble those bridges
3. The construction of the Light Horse Interchange (which connects the M7 with the M4) — the largest of its type in the southern hemisphere.

The bridges were Jurd's first problem. Early on the consortium discovered that there was not enough manufacturing capacity on the east coast to build the bridges needed. It was a turning point for the project.

"I remember the meeting clearly," he said. "We were sitting there dumbstruck and you realise you have to think bigger. So we decided that we had to build our own factory to build the bridges, most of which required pre-cast, pre-stressed concrete girders." The ten-hectare factory cost more than A\$20 million. The interchange had to be constructed around existing roads without disturbing traffic. The consortium successfully completed that facet of the project, which included 18 bridges (and 802 bridge segments in the interchange). There were also eight ramps connecting the M7 to the M4, and the interchange is 23 metres above the M4 at its highest point. This is a great illustration of finishing strong. Like David Jurd, we must not allow the 'impossibilities' to overcome us. As Jurd said, "Anything is possible!"

Choose the right attitude

To finish strongly, you need a great attitude. Author Chuck Swindoll said:

> *I believe the single most significant decision I can make on a day-to-day basis is my choice of attitude... When my attitudes are right, there is no barrier too high, no valley too deep, no dream too extreme, no challenge too great for me.*

To develop and maintain a great attitude, you need to take charge of your emotions, you need to focus on what's good and reject anything that makes you petty and a bitter person.

There have been many times in the history of Gloria Jean's Coffees when giving up seemed the easiest way out. In the early days we faced financial cash flow issues and we experienced stressful times when employees or franchisees disappointed us. We felt like giving up when everything seemed to go wrong at 4.30pm on Friday... and when we were tired, sick or worried about family members. At these times everything can look bad; your mind tends to recall all the problems, digging you deeper and deeper into a pit. At these times you feel it isn't worthwhile going on. In our case, each time we felt this way we made a conscious choice to look at the bigger picture. We focused on all the wins and successes. We ignored the feelings ('fake it till you make it' is a good standby) and we handed all our problems to God, because He can handle it far better than we can!

Jerry Seinfeld expressed an interesting take on life when he stated:

Life is truly a ride. We're all strapped in, and no one can stop it. When the doctor slaps your behind, he's ripping your ticket and away you go. As you make each passage from youth to adulthood to maturity, sometimes you put your arms up and scream, sometimes you just hang on to the bar in front of you. But the ride is the thing. I think the most you can hope for at the end of life is that your hair's messed up, you're out of breath, and you didn't throw up.

Personally, I want more from life than this. Like most people, I want my life to make a difference, to be significant, and I want to leave a good example for my family to follow. I want to finish strong!

take action | NOW!

one: Focus on endurance over speed, so pace yourself over the long haul.

two: The journey with a large vision will take time and, in many cases, could take a lifetime. Therefore there will need to be regular benchmarks where your achievements are celebrated and rewarded along the journey.

three: Develop and maintain a great attitude.

four: Don't be afraid to try new things. Here are four ways to overcome fear:
- Tackle fear head on.
- Hang out with courageous people.
- Take courage and go for it!
- Believe you can finish strongly.

five: Never give up. If you feel like you want to give up…
- Ask yourself, *Am I still passionate about my business, my job or my relationship?* If not, then make a decision to re-kindle the passion. Invest time in yourself with motivational teaching, seminars, books and CDs.
- Focus on the positive aspects of what you are doing, the good reports and achievements.
- Remind yourself several times a day of your vision, mission and values.
- Don't be afraid to ask for help and encouragement—the only thing you stand to lose is your pride.

eleven | STOP AND CHANGE WHEN NECESSARY

If the horse is dead, dismount

"Two basic rules of life: 1. Change is Inevitable 2. Everyone Resists Change. Remember this: When you are through changing... you're through."
Source unknown

You will never make it to your vision if you keep doing things that don't work. When we started Gloria Jean's Coffees, it seemed a great concept. The coffee was certainly an excellent product, but the focus of the concept (with a large emphasis on coffee and tea related merchandise), and some of the systems (for example, the standards manuals and training were outdated and inadequate) were not helping us to grow and become successful. Whilst we decided that some of the methods and actions needed to change, we determined that our vision must not change. We reviewed our business and realised that what we brought over from the USA—the brand and the product—had great potential. All the elements for success existed, however they were badly followed through in the USA. And their lack of development was not helping us.

So we decided we needed to review the specialty coffee market, and we started to make some changes. The store designs changed from gift stores to specialty coffee outlets with seating and large pastry cabinets. Training programs were improved and extended, manuals updated and enhanced, franchisee support and marketing programs improved. We took a high quality product and introduced our own system to make it a success.

You've probably heard the old Dakota Indian tribal saying, "If the horse is dead, dismount!" If your business is not going anywhere, you may need to get out of whatever it is you are doing... or make some drastic changes! Are you sitting on business practices, products or services that really need to be changed? Some industries are notorious for hanging on to programs and systems that are no longer relevant. Why do we cling to practices, products and programs that aren't working? Well, it's usually because of fear. We often have a fear of what our friends may think or what our family may think. Sometimes it's simply a fear of change. So make the necessary changes now so that you can move forward.

Don't be frightened to make a mistake

Thomas Edison failed 2000 times before he finally got the electric light bulb working. His friends told him, "You failed 2000 times."
He said, "No, I found 2000 ways that won't work!"

Now that's a different attitude!

We often need to put aside what our family, friends and business associates think. If you're going to be a leader—like Edison—then you are going to have to constantly innovate and not be frightened to make a mistake. When leaders make mistakes, they quickly bounce back up and get back on track. Edison bounced back 2000 times.

There were times during my last two years as managing director of DDB Needham Advertising when our board of directors made decisions that weren't achieving the desired results. My response at the time was, "Well, let's stop and change direction. It's not working. Let's move on!"
"You can't do that!" some of the directors would reply. "What will people think?!"
"They'll think worse of us if we continue down this path," I replied. "But if we change direction now and get it right, what people think won't even be an issue."

For many, change is too difficult

It's easy not to make the tough decisions to change. It's more comfortable to just drift along if most things are working well. But don't accept the mindset that close enough is good enough. We should *do* the best and *be* the best in everything we do. And often that will mean change and it will mean work. The reason people sometimes don't want to change is simple—it is hard! It is actually easier to keep the status quo than to change. As they say, "No pain, no gain."

When we changed to a new business software package at the support office of Gloria Jean's Coffees—one that would give us far better reporting and more streamlined data entry—some of our staff at the time found it easier to continue using their old spreadsheets. This meant that data was not collected correctly and was not included in the new system. Numbers were not quite the same coming from the old spreadsheets and some variables were left out entirely. Time was wasted doing everything twice and mistakes crept in. It isn't always easy to learn how to use an upgraded system, however the benefits far outweigh the difficulty. If we had continued using the original software programs, there is no way we would have been able to develop or grow the business. Unfortunately, people often operate in their own comfort zone, not willing to stretch. This will stall your business growth and progress.

If you want to grow, you need to change

In our businesses, if we want to grow we need to develop a 'culture of change' in which there is no fear or feeling of insecurity when change occurs. As part of a large and rapidly growing church, some years ago I remember our pastor saying many times, "If you want to make this your church, you will have to get used to change, because nothing will stay the same for long." And he was right! As the church grew, we often moved from one rented building to another. Even in our large new facility today, many of us battle to get the most convenient car park space or the best seat in the auditorium. (I often joke that I have tried virtually every car park space and every seat in the new auditorium). Structures and programs have had to change many times to accommodate the growth.

This has also been the case at Gloria Jean's Coffees. We have some long-term staff who will tell you they have had at least six different desks in one of the two buildings we occupy. We need to prepare our people for growth by constantly communicating our achievements and our future expectations so that our staff are neither surprised nor fearful of our growth. At Gloria Jean's Coffees, we will continue to work as though we are in transit lounges, not fixed abodes.

There have been times when we have deleted drinks from our menu board and removed bean varieties from our whole bean selection. In the early days, one of the first changes was to take the Malted Mocha Chiller off our menu board. It had been rating very poorly in cold drink sales and our newer, more popular drinks were to be added to the menu. Comments from one or two of our franchisees indicated they were shocked at this change because they considered this drink very important in their store sales mix (even though they had only been selling one or two per month). But once the change was made, the negative comments vanished. And in our stores nationwide customers hardly noticed the change. The new drinks soon out-performed the old one! These days our franchisees look forward to the introduction of new drinks to their menu. They expect and anticipate changes to the menu board knowing that it boosts their sales.

Make adjustments when plans go wrong

Effective leaders are able to adjust when plans go wrong or when results don't turn out the way they expect. Successful business people also remain teachable; they are willing to change if it means a more successful outcome.

How about you? Are you flexible enough to change plans when necessary? Or do you find yourself justifying your current results when you know you can do better? Do you find yourself rejecting new ideas and innovations simply because you are comfortable? If so, you need to consider how committed you are to a spirit of excellence and to achieving your vision. If you *are* committed to change for the better, then begin to listen to valid customer criticism and staff feedback and decide if they have merit. They may point to systems, practices or even products and services that aren't working and from which you may need to 'dismount' your dead or dying horse.

Even though changes and adjustments may sometimes be necessary, mature leaders and business people are also able to maintain perspective, especially when things don't go according to plan. So let me encourage you to continue to see the bigger picture and focus on the vision, because this will help you see past the mistakes that are inevitable in any organisation. Whilst your vision doesn't change, some of your products, services or systems may need to. Your products, services and systems may not be bad or ineffective in themselves, but they may not help you reach your vision.

In everything you do, whether in your relationships with your family, church, business or sporting group, be willing to do the best you can. Be willing to challenge the concept that close enough is good enough. Be prepared to get rid of practices, services and products that aren't working. Set yourself on course to reach the vision you established at the very beginning.

George Bernard Shaw once declared, "Progress is impossible without change." Sometimes change simply means improvements to products or adjustments to programs. Other times it may be necessary to change your direction completely.

If you do, remember that once you set your sails in a new direction, you are no longer hopelessly blown by the winds of impulse, circumstance, expediency, popular opinion or self-interest. And once you set your new direction, be sure to enjoy the journey.

take action | NOW!

one: Constantly innovate and don't be afraid to make mistakes.

two: Develop a 'culture of change' in your organisation so that there is no fear when change occurs.

three: Be prepared to adjust when plans go wrong or when results don't turn out the way you had expected.

four: Remain teachable and flexible enough to change plans when necessary.

five: Maintain perspective, continue to see the bigger picture, and focus on the vision — this will help you see past the mistakes that are inevitable in any organization.

six: Ask yourself these questions:
- Do I have products, services, programs or attitudes from which I need to 'dismount'?
- Am I operating in a comfortable space?
- Am I ready to step out, bear the pain that comes with gain, and claim the future?

twelve | IN TRAVELLING THROUGH LIFE, TRAVEL LIGHT

Don't let the problems of the past weigh you down

"Resentment or grudges do no harm to the person against whom you hold these feelings, but every day and every night of your life, they are eating at you."
Norman Vincent Peale

Danish philosopher Soren Kierkegaard once stated, "Life can only be understood backwards, but it must be lived forwards." I can only share my experiences with you by looking back over ten years at Gloria Jean's Coffees and more than 30 years at DDB Needham Advertising. To be honest, it's easy to just chat about your life in a book like this, but you can only actually share your experiences when you've really lived them. And the lessons I've learned as I experience life are sometimes only recognised and understood much later.

As we travel through life, you and I need to learn to collect the good things in our lives and learn from them, but we must be careful not to collect bad attitudes along the way. A chip on the shoulder becomes a very heavy load. It will weigh you down, weigh your business down, and weigh your relationships down.

In my advertising days I worked with many people who could not forgive or forget. Their 'chip on the shoulder' slowed their progress, and eventually dominated their thinking. They became ineffective, which limited their job opportunities and their future. Their health suffered and, in some cases, they started to drink to excess.

Don't let the sun go down on your anger

Jealousy of colleagues and bitterness over competitors become a very heavy load. So does watching over your shoulder all the time and digging up the past. You've got to learn to bury the past and move on. Don't dwell on the past. The apostle Paul once said, "Don't let the sun go down on your anger." (Ephesians 4:27) We need to deal with situations quickly so that they don't eat away at us, gnaw away at our business, and slowly destroy our relationships.

There have been occasions when people have sent me emails criticising me or personally attacking me. Over the last three years there have been a few antagonistic emails, letters and telephone calls demanding I confirm that Gloria Jean's Coffees is owned by my church, Hillsong Church in Sydney. My emphatic reply has always been, "No, but why would it matter if it did?" Perhaps some feel this would bring discredit on the church, or that the business somehow financially profits from the church. The important thing is that I have not let this weigh me down.

I once spoke at a business forum and then spent over an hour answering questions one-on-one with delegates. About a month later I received an email from someone who had attended that forum. He told me he was disappointed in me because I had been too busy to talk to him during the time I had spent one-on-one with delegates. He came to the conclusion that I had not respected him at that event. After reading the email, I called him to find out how I had upset him and soon discovered that he had been standing back behind the crowd; he had not actually come forward for me to see him or talk to him. So to claim that I had ignored him was not correct. By quickly calling him, I was able to bring some resolution to the matter.

On another occasion a franchisee accused me of not being interested in him or his store. He also claimed that our support office staff never helped him. We soon realised that there was no substantiation for his comments. In fact, when I reviewed the history of our dealings with this franchisee, the support office staff had gone way beyond what was expected in assisting this franchisee. Those who know me are also aware that I would regularly visit our stores and provide input into franchisees' businesses. I always followed up on any outstanding matters. This franchisee had a chip on his shoulder that needed to be dealt with. It was affecting his relationship with the support office, and this was impacting on his business.

I've learned that when something gets the blood boiling, it's better to wait until the next day before responding. My response is always delivered better the next day than in the heat of the moment. The temptation is to give as good as you get, to respond vindictively or bitterly. But this only escalates the situation, causing unnecessary conflict. Responding in a balanced way reduces the potential for it to escalate into a much worse situation and eventually both parties can move forward successfully. I write and deliver better responses when I wait.

The fact is that we often only get half the story first. We have all been guilty of reacting strongly to some issue, only to find that the person we blamed was not actually at fault. So when you next find yourself in that situation, wait… and then ask the right questions.

Don't carry emotional baggage around with you. Unfortunately there have been times when we've taken on franchisees who have had unresolved prior emotional baggage and all they've done is create a disaster in their relationships and with their own staff. They have the potential to become great franchisees, but at that point in time they were not ready for it. There have even been instances when our franchisees have experienced jealousy from other retailers in their shopping centre. Their drink posters were destroyed, stock went missing, milk delivery containers were punctured with holes, and nasty rumours were spread. These types of attitudes in a retailer only serve to drive customers away. Most of us enjoy a store where there is a positive, friendly atmosphere. I have seen competitors lose customers because of the obvious negativity shown towards our franchisees. They destroy their own businesses because they focus on other people's businesses.

Initiate reconciliation in relationships

On the other hand, we have had a number of franchisees who have been determined to build relationships with their 'perceived' competition, as well as with other retailers in their location. In every case, these franchisees have become respected and loved by customers. They have built very successful stores with loyal customers and staff because their attitude has been attractive. Remember, positive attitudes attract positive responses. And even if competitors and customers don't respond positively, at least you know you have done your best.

Learn to initiate reconciliation in any situation. Don't wait for someone else to initiate reconciliation for you. In the end, it doesn't really matter who is at fault—the sooner the strife is cleared up, the smoother business will run. People with a lot of emotional baggage make very slow progress. If you want to move forward and grow your business, you will need to get rid of those bags!

Insecurity also creates problems. When we have an inner security and a healthy self-esteem, it provides a foundation for strong leadership. But when we are insecure, we start to drift from our vision as soon as problems arise or people stop liking us or finances slow down. When morale dips or when others criticise us, we start to crumble if we don't feel secure. These feelings will eventually sabotage our leadership and destroy our business.

In our early years at Gloria Jean's Coffees, we were criticised by the coffee industry and by many people who didn't understand the Gloria Jean's Coffees concept and system. Today we don't have the same level of criticism (except from those who don't understand franchising or the speciality coffee market). That criticism could have stopped our growth, but it didn't… because we believed in ourselves.

Author John Maxwell once stated that the following symptoms usually indicate feelings of insecurity:
1. **Comparison** – we compare ourselves with others and keep score
2. **Compensation** – we feel like a victim and must compensate

for our losses
3. **Competition** – we become self-consumed and try to outdo others for attention
4. **Compulsion** – we feel driven to perform in order to gain others' approval
5. **Condemnation** – we judge others or ourselves, resulting in self-pity or conceit
6. **Control** – we feel we must take charge, protect our interest and manipulate.

Step out from beyond what you can see

Insecurity comes in many subtle forms and holds us back far too often. Many of us need to take more risks in order to move forward in business and relationships. Sometimes we must step out in faith. When we are working with what we can already see—something that is already in operation or established—we usually don't feel the need to take any risks. The problem is that we can't see very far; we can only see the business performing either at the same level or just a little better than it is at present. Living by sight keeps us living small.

I often ask business people where they would like their business to be in five years. Then I get them to start developing a yearly plan to reach their goal. With this in place, I find people start to become excited. They finally see their plans as achievable and obstacles don't knock them over as easily.

The reason many of us can't develop in our businesses or in our relationships is that we can't reach beyond our line of sight. We need to take a step of faith to develop a big vision. We need to exercise faith to be able to step out from beyond what we can see in front of us right now. Our limited vision is holding us back.

The impala is a swift-running antelope found in central and southern Africa. In one jump it can soar 2.5 metres (eight feet) high and nine metres (30 feet) in distance. And yet it has one unique limitation. You can place an impala in a cage with one-metre high walls and no roof and it will not attempt to escape, even though it has more than enough ability to clear the cage! The impala's flaw is that it won't jump if it cannot see where its feet will land. The impala lives and operates by sight, so it's easy to keep caged and controlled. We're the same! We won't jump if we can't see where we will land. Imagine where your business could be if you didn't simply rely on what you see now! So shrug off the insecurities and inhibitions that have held you back so far.

I have spent quite a lot of time visiting franchisees in their stores. After the initial "Hi!" some will say, "I've been talking to all the other retailers in the centre and they are saying the centre's foot traffic is down 20 percent due to shopping centre renovations." Or they will tell me, "Things are slow this week because a new mall has opened nearby." The first thing I *do* is get them to look outside their store or I take them for a walk around the centre. Then the first thing I *say* is, "Take a look around you. Foot traffic may be down, but 80 percent of people are still coming through the doors. What can you do to attract these customers to your store?"

At Gloria Jean's Coffees, we have an LSM (Local Store Marketing) program to build customer store traffic. In each store situation, there are many innovative ideas to adopt which would suit the location and style of business. For instance, rather than worrying about other retailers and their rumours, and instead of sitting in the comfort zone of the store environment, go out and attract customers! I encourage franchisees to be innovative in approach and to make their store a fun, enjoyable place to be in. In other words, step out beyond what you can see right now.

A victim mentality can also stunt your growth. Never regret the hard lessons or the difficult relationships you have to negotiate in life; you need to learn from them. But don't develop a victim mentality. All of us have ample opportunity to blame others for problems and failures, often with justification. And I am certainly no different. But I firmly believe that one of the reasons for the success of Gloria Jean's Coffees has been our conscious determination not to live with a victim attitude, not to let the problems of the past dictate our future, and not to hold onto grudges, bitterness or regret—whether with staff, franchisees, suppliers or customers. As American folk singer and songwriter Joan Baez once said, "You don't get to choose how you're going to die, or when. You can only decide how you're going to live now." So live life to the full and live it forwards. You won't regret it!

take action | NOW!

one: Collect the good things along your life's journey and learn from them, and be careful not to collect bad attitudes along the way.

two: Don't dwell on past mistakes or painful memories. Don't let the sun go down on your anger. Deal with situations quickly so that they don't destroy your relationships.

three: Become a person who initiates reconciliation in relationships. Positive attitudes attract positive responses.

four: Nurture a healthy self-esteem—it will keep you focused on your vision despite what people say and do to you.

five: Exercise faith to step out from beyond what you can see immediately in front of you. Learn to take a risk and jump, even when you can't see where you will land.

thirteen |

MINDSETS

Don't live in other people's mindsets

"I succeed on my own personal motivation, dedication and commitment. My mindset is: If I'm not out there training, someone else is."
Lynn Jennings (Olympic distance runner)

Mindsets will determine your success. Whether it's your own mindset or the mindsets of those around you, limited thinking will hold you ransom to limited achievements. On the other hand, a healthy mindset will set you up for success in every area of your life and business.

Bodybuilder, actor and politician Arnold Schwarzenegger once declared:

"The mind is the limit. As long as the mind can envision the fact that you can do something, you can do it – as long as you really believe 100 percent. It's all mind over matter. All I know is that the first step is to create the vision, because when you see the vision there – that creates the want power. For example, my wanting to be Mr Universe came about because I saw myself so clearly, being up there on the stage winning".

Unfortunately, in life and in business many people will tell you what you *can't* do. These people are revealing their own limited thinking, or in some cases they may be operating from their own comfort zones. Their small mindsets haven't been stretched or enlarged. So when you decide to do something different or risky, like launching a product, changing a service, or establishing a larger vision, you'll find at least ten percent of people will either oppose you or disagree with you.

Based on my experiences at Gloria Jean's Coffees and McDonald's, let me give you seven examples of mindsets to avoid:

Landlord mindsets: Landlords, especially in our early years, believe Gloria Jean's Coffees stores can afford to pay excessively high rents. This attitude is not isolated to the specialist coffee sector; it extends to all retail sectors. Landlords' expectations are not based on what the market is paying in rent, but on the number of people entering the stores. They seem to believe that a cup of coffee has a large margin, so when they see the high foot traffic going through our stores it paints an incorrect picture.

At Gloria Jean's Coffees we have had to educate landlords that the cost of a cup of coffee is small, and that our stores need to have a large number of transactions to be able to pay rent, labour, COGs (cost of goods), operating costs, financing… and then make some money at the end. Any profit at each of our stores requires a substantial number of customers walking through the store. It also requires a franchisee to be managing their cost of goods and labour well, and to be delivering a great in-store experience and quality of product. This is something that landlords have difficulty understanding. (I guess they always will because they are after a return on their investment.) This wrong mindset directly impacts on the viability of retail businesses.

Accountant and lawyer mindsets: Many accountants and lawyers have wrong mindsets. There are many in these professions who have old-fashioned ideas and have never moved with the times in the way business is conducted today. Unfortunately, many of them don't understand franchising. They view franchising in terms of a traditional business model. Because of this limited thinking, they give bad advice to clients.
Shopfitter mindsets: Shopfitters will often say to us, "That can't be done!" At Gloria Jean's Coffees, we have had experiences with both good shopfitters and bad shopfitters. They are all well intentioned, but this is very much an undisciplined industry. I found from my experience working in advertising that television

production companies operated at a similar level: They charged the maximum price to produce a television commercial, but there was little accountability. The people working in these companies would spend unnecessary money on changes to a television commercial long before the client had seen it and approved the extra expenditure. This resulted in bad relationships with clients.

The shopfitter mindset is one of short-sighted planning. Many shopfitters run on the smell of an oily rag. (In some cases, I am sure there is no oil on the rag at all!) In their industry, everything is last-minute. Sometimes stores are fitted out with little planning, despite the fact that they know they will have limited time on site. I have seen shopfitters go out of business because they run their cash flow so tight they need to move onto the next job to be able to pay the bills for the last shop fit-out. At Gloria Jean's Coffees, we had to set the shopfitters' disciplines in place ourselves in order to get what we paid for in the time we had allocated. Shopfitters who said to us, "That can't be done!" soon began to learn that at Gloria Jean's Coffees we have a can-do, professional mindset. Today we continue to face issues in which items still need to be finalized after the store has opened. This is why it is important to retain the last payment until all work is completed and signed off.

Competitor mindsets: In the chapter on Marketing, I have already addressed the problem in which competitors often copy each other's advertising strategies or ideas. It's far better to be a leader in your industry and let everyone follow you.

When Gloria Jean's Coffees commenced operations in Australia, we often introduced a new innovation, a new whole bean variety, or a new drink. What we found in the early days was that it would take two or three years before there was any acknowledgment from a competitor about what we were doing. These days I believe it's a matter of months before our drinks or ideas are copied. That's life today for most product and service categories, unless you launch a 'way-out-of-left-field' idea. The copycat mindset is well entrenched today.

We introduced the frequent sippers card when we first started our business. Back then no one in the coffee industry utilized this idea. Today almost everyone has a frequent user card in some form. Today you can find loyalty reward cards everywhere, from bakery shops (where you can buy five loaves of bread and get one free) to film developing (where you can pay for five films to be developed and get the next one free). These rewards cards have become an icon... not something we set out to do! Believe it or not, when we launched our frequent sippers card concept, we were told it wouldn't work. Another wrong mindset!

We introduced into our drinks flavoured syrups, such as Hazelnut, French Vanilla, Swiss Chocolate Almond and Irish Crème. At the time, we were in an industry in which distributors had flavoured syrups gathering dust in warehouses. Today you can walk into almost every restaurant, café or coffee shop and order a variety of flavours in your coffee. However, the problem with flavours is that the quality varies. In some instances, the flavours are not designed for this purpose, so they tend to overpower the actual coffee and they may even disguise poor quality coffee beans. These competitors are copycats, not innovators or leaders.

When we started introducing two or three-seater lounges and tub lounges into our stores to create a relaxed atmosphere, we were on our own. Today many coffee outlets, bookshops and other venues have introduced lounges to help people relax and enjoy the surrounding environment. Realistically, there can never be enough lounges for everyone to sit on; they help create an atmosphere of warmth and comfort. But stores still need to create maximum seating to allow for the amount of rent being paid. Coffee stores that copy this concept and provide mostly lounge seating not only find it rather expensive to fit out, they also find it difficult to fit customers in, because if they don't get the seating ratio right they may struggle to pay the rent.

We introduced chai tea as a drink in Australia in 2000. It was not generally known back then. Now you can find chai tea with varying degrees of quality in almost every café and restaurant. Today it's also available in supermarkets! Again, we were told it wouldn't sell in Australia. Another wrong mindset and another lost opportunity for others.

McDonald's introduced the hash brown as a breakfast menu item when it launched its breakfast menu in Australia. (Hash browns were not traditionally eaten in this country back then.) Now hash browns are available almost everywhere, even at the breakfast buffet in high-class hotels and in supermarkets. McDonald's was criticized when it launched hash browns in its restaurants. Another example of a limited mindset!

In 2003 we launched our involvement in support of a charity called Mercy Ministries. We set up cash donation boxes in every store. Some people saw only the problems with this partnership arrangement. They had a miserly mindset. "This is too difficult!" they stated. "Who is to collect and bank the coins?" they complained. "And how will this benefit the business?" (I should say that these comments did *not* come from our franchisees, who were overwhelmingly supportive.)

Today you will find that many coffee chains have introduced charity partnerships to their operations. I don't have a problem with this. In fact, I believe our leadership in this area has benefited us along with many others. If you want your business or industry to grow and you show the kind of leadership that others will follow, then you should be innovating and you should be creating a quality difference. I firmly believe the leader gets the bulk share of the market, while those who follow may still grow but they will continue to maintain a smaller share of the market.

The other problem in copying a competitor is that you don't know if what they've introduced is working. There were times when we didn't have great success with some of the products we introduced and we have consequently stopped selling those particular products. Any competitor copying these products would have made the same mistake.

Media mindsets: The media always wants to generate stories with attention-grabbing headlines. You can present the facts to reporters and they can still publish or broadcast stories that are totally contradictory. To them, contradiction and controversy are what make great stories, and what sells magazines and newspapers, and what attracts viewers and listeners.

The media also has been great at helping build the coffee industry and in educating the market. In some cases the media has even slowly begun to understand the franchise industry. However, for some time there have been individual members of the media who have been negative about national coffee chains and franchising. They can be critical of your business (especially if you stand up and do something different in the market), they can be critical of you personally, and they can be critical of your industry.

Unfortunately, many reporters change jobs, which means that once you appear to have educated a reporter they move on and you have to begin educating the new reporter who is trying to make his or her mark. So much for quality journalism! So don't build your business on the media mindset. Don't build your business on what the media do or do not say about you, your business or your industry. The media mindset is driven by the need to get attention, sometimes despite the truth.

Family, friends and colleagues mindsets: There are so many people close to you who will tell you what you can't do. They have mindsets about you and your business. When we purchased the international rights for the Gloria Jean's Coffees brand (and the supply) and signed the agreement in 2005, some of the comments we received were:

"You can't run that from Australia!"
"What about the different cultures and customs?"
"What about the languages?"
"What about the distance?"
"How are you going to supervise it?"
"How are you going to protect your brand?"
"What about government regulations?"

All these comments and cautions were valid. They were right that the risks were very high, but we went ahead and did it anyway, despite the mindsets. We have been able to open Gloria Jean's Coffees in more than 30 countries (at current count). We have a brand that is growing internationally. We have done all the things we were told we couldn't do. Yes, there are issues and there are obstacles. Yes, there are mountains to climb. But it's the same in every business and in every situation. Watch out for any family, friends and business associate mindsets that tell you what cannot be done.

Research mindsets: The co-founder of advertising firm Doyle Dane Bernbach International, Bill Bernbach, once stated: "We are so busy measuring public opinion that we forget we can mold it. We are so busy listening to statistics we forget we can create them." (I also quoted this statement in the Marketing chapter.) Research will give you mindsets from your customers. Research will inform you what customers currently know *today* and what they are comfortable with *today*. The challenge is that these days very few people seem to innovate or show vision for the future growth of their product or category. Therefore we need to go out and innovate. We need to go out and create our own statistics.

When we commenced our first Gloria Jean's Coffees store in mid-November 1996, we were told by people in the coffee industry that the concept wouldn't work. We were told that people wouldn't drink flavoured coffees. We were told that they wouldn't buy their coffee in a takeaway cup. In the end, through our determination and in some ways our naivety, Australian attitudes to drinking coffee and tea have changed dramatically. The coffee industry itself has benefited from the surge in business, not only with coffee beans and tea, but also through quality hot chocolates and through coffee flavourings. Certainly the industry is far in excess of where it was when we started. This is not something we intentionally set out to do, but it was something that occurred and turned the industry on its ear.

If you are going to listen to all the people who tell you what you can and can't do, you will never do anything. The great American writer and philosopher Henry David Thoreau wisely said, "Things do not change; we change." You need to go out and do something different. American computer scientist Alan Kay once declared, "Don't worry about what anybody else is going to do." I also like what artist and cartoonist Saul Steinberg said:

"The best way to predict the future is to invent it." You need to do that in your *industry*. You need to do that in your business, product or service *category*. And you need to learn to actually do that in your own *business*.

There will always be obstacles and opposition to overcome. There will always be difficulties and mountains to plough through. Decide right now that you won't live in other people's mindsets. Only when you make that decision will you give yourself the best chance to achieve your dreams.

take action | NOW!

one: Watch out for landlord mindsets; landlords are focused only on a return on their investment. Make the effort to educate them about your business or service so that they see the need for flexibility.

two: Be wary of accountant and lawyer mindsets that have old-fashioned ideas, never move with the times, and give bad advice to clients. Look for service suppliers who have a superior knowledge of your product, service, business and industry.

three: Shopfitter mindsets will tell you, "That can't be done!" Ignore them! Adopt a can-do mindset instead.

four: Don't be put off by competitor or copycat mindsets. There are great advantages to being a leader in an industry. I believe the leader gets the bulk share of the market anyway. So lead the way!

five: Don't take notice of media mindsets that, for the most part, will be critical of your business. Instead, watch for opportunities to use the media to your advantage, to build demand for your product, service, business or industry.

six: Watch out for family, friends and colleagues mindsets that will try to tell you what you can't do. Go ahead and do it anyway!

seven: Avoid a research mindset that bases everything on public opinion. Remember that you can mold public opinion; you can create products and services that people do not yet know they want or need.

eight: Above all, determine to maintain healthy mindsets.

fourteen

NEGATIVITY

Negative attitudes can sabotage your future

"It takes but one positive thought when given a chance to survive and thrive to overpower an entire army of negative thoughts."
Robert H. Schuller

American peace activist, Peace Pilgrim, once stated, "If you realized how powerful your thoughts are, you would never think a negative thought." Whether positive or negative, our thoughts and attitudes are powerful. They can destroy and they can create. The success of your business and your relationships very much depends on your attitude to life: Are you a positive or a negative person?

I have noticed that even the most positive people can be blindsided by negativity. Negative attitudes can creep up on us in many ways. Sometimes the approach is subtle. At other times negativity can jump right out at us. Sometimes negativity can begin as small thoughts. And at other times negativity can begin instantly as very bad news.

Small things like 'sharing' negative opinions about other people can create divisions between people. My Wife Sue well remembers hearing a former employee sharing negative opinions about certain franchisees with other staff members. This was soon confronted, but many people simply don't realize the damage this can do. The members of our staff at Gloria Jean's Coffees are a team. So neither support staff nor franchisees can survive without pulling together as a team. If we destroy each other with words, we create a divisive 'us and them' attitude which breeds more and more negative, critical comment.

At times we have also had people working with us whose character tended towards the negative. Almost anything that happened became a tragedy. Every time you visited their workstation you would come away feeling the world had come to an end, that there was no hope. I would brace myself before speaking to these people and avoid asking any questions that required their opinion!

More often than not, negativity creeps up on us without us realizing it. For instance, there are a few old sayings that may seem rather harmless, but they influence us in very negative ways. Most of us would have heard the saying, "Ignorance is bliss." Another one is, "What you don't know won't hurt you." The reality is that these sayings are rubbish and they are dangerous! Ignorance should never be accepted. What these sayings tell us is that there is nothing wrong with ignorance. But you and I know better than that! Whether you are a leader in your organisation, or you run a business, or you are an employee in a business, the expectation is that if you don't know something, you ask; if you don't know how to do something, then you find out.

In contrast to these sayings, what you don't know *can* jump out and hurt you. Your ignorance *can* clobber you along your journey. Surprises and challenges will always fall across our path — that's life! But if we strive to be all that we can be and absorb as much knowledge as we can, then we will be better prepared to deal with life's surprises.

I often find that it is not the large negative thoughts that actually affect my future, it's usually the small ones. Small, almost insignificant negative thoughts, if left to fester, will do immense damage. They will attack your vision and your focus. They will come at you from within yourself and they will be passed on from business associates, family, friends and the media. Little doubts niggle away at our confidence and self-esteem. Small thoughts of jealousy or bitterness eat away at our positive attitude to life. In my advertising days there were many instances where one negative comment about a staff member, or even a client, created a flow-on effect, growing into a major backlash. On at least two occasions the negative comment got back to the client or staff member with extreme reactions.

Deal swiftly with negativity

If we want to be successful in business and in relationships, we need to learn to deal with this issue of destructive negative thoughts and attitudes. Negativity needs to be dealt with swiftly because it will defeat you if you don't meet it head on. Like weeds that start small and spindly in your garden, negativity can grow and spread quickly if you don't pay attention to it. Once it grows, it will knock you over, it will slow you down, and it will stop you from reaching your goals.

Most of us seem to be easily influenced by negative thoughts, by negative attitudes, and by negative comments from other people. There are periods of time when we are more vulnerable to negativity. I find the negative thoughts justify themselves and have more effect on me when I have had a busy day and when I am physically and mentally tired.

Have you ever wondered why it's usually in the middle of the night that a negative thought builds into a mammoth mountain? It is often when everything is quiet, when there are no distractions, when we are tired and weary, that negativity runs wild. An exhausted, overworked mind is fertile ground for a harvest of negativity.

Many years ago, a comment was made that a particular television media 'buy' our department had made was a poor one. This was based on incorrect information. This negative comment directly affected me, so much so that during the following night I had worked myself into the belief that the agency would lose the account and I would lose my job. Overnight, the whole world had fallen in! Of course morning came and life went on as usual, because I had the opportunity to answer and correct the comment that had been made.

Challenges often make us more vulnerable to negativity. When a person who has just purchased a business goes through difficult times, that person will very quickly adopt a defeated attitude. Once people get to this stage, nothing is seen from a positive perspective. Indecision creeps in and the 'little things' become major obstacles. Unless these moments are dealt with and put into true perspective, they will finally affect that person's business and relationships. So be prepared for these moments. Be wary of negative thoughts when you face periods of challenge and growth.

Senior Pastor of Hillsong Church in Sydney, Brian Houston, is a great believer in controlling negative thoughts before they can do some damage. He once stated: "Negativity can be one of the most destructive forces in our lives... Sadly, human nature has a tendency to sink into a negative way of thinking, so we all need to learn how to challenge negativity daily." He shared some of the following thoughts on how you and I can daily tackle negativity:

1) *Negativity always reflects inner defeat*
The words we speak become a reflection of what is in our head and our heart. Jesus said in Matthew chapter 12, "Out of the abundance of the heart the mouth speaks." This is so true. We need to be careful of the words we speak, especially when we are tired, down and defeated. After realizing we have just said something negative, we often say, "I didn't mean that!" In fact, we did, because if we said it, then it's usually a reflection of what we have been thinking. A verse in the book of Proverbs says, "What you think in your heart, so you are." (Proverbs 23:7) So be careful what you say, because whatever you are thinking and feeling will be reflected through your words.

2) *Negativity will always try to justify itself*
When we have a negative attitude towards someone, we start to justify within ourselves that we are in the right and that they are in the wrong. Reality becomes distorted. Negative mindsets dictate their own reality. We believe that no one is on our side, that no one wants to help us, that we are on our own, that our business is dead, and that our relationships are doomed to failure. And

our negative mindsets give us the reasons why this is so. When negativity builds up momentum in our minds, it's hard to stop. This is another very strong reason to nip negativity in the bud before it establishes root in our minds.

I have spent time with people who completely justify their negative reactions. They often come across as genuine and long-suffering; they are this way because of some tragedy or illness in their lives, because of some burden they continue to bear. They are no doubt right—many are affected by tragic circumstances. However, there also are many who choose not to let these circumstances rule them, and who make a decision to react in the positive rather than the negative. These people don't give negativity a chance to grow.

3) *Negativity will choose your friends for you*

As human beings, our nature is to gather around us people of a similar mind. So when we are down, we want people around us who are going to sympathize with us, who are going to encourage that negativity. When we believe that someone is trying to harm us, we gather around us other business people, family or friends who will actually feed that negativity and confirm for us that someone is out to get us.

At a Gloria Jean's Coffees franchise meeting a few years ago, as Sue was mixing with the crowd during a lunch break, she joined a rather negative conversation between two people. Within a short space of time, the discussion between the two became an intense one-on-one about their varied health woes. The focused negativity attracted the two people together in such a powerful way that they did not notice that Sue had joined them and they didn't notice when she left.

To break negative mindsets, we need to find positive people; we need to spend time with people who have experienced success and let them speak into our lives. We need to allow the positive outlook of those around us to permeate us and to counter the negative attitudes. The Book of Proverbs says that he who walks with the wise, grows wise, but a companion of fools suffers harm. (Proverbs 13:20) So choose your friends wisely, for they will influence your mindsets and affect the level of your success.

4) *Negativity distorts the truth*

As I have said before, negativity distorts the truth. A negative mindset only sees the bad, but the words of a positive person will lighten your situation. The Book of Proverbs says that an anxious heart weighs a man down, but a kind word cheers him up. (Proverbs 12:25) Being able to provide positive input and encourage someone actually stops the truth being distorted. You and I are able to guide the influence of negativity in our own lives and in other people's lives by putting situations into proper perspective. We can limit the damaging effects of a negative mindset by not allowing ourselves and others to magnify the problem beyond reality.

When I worked in advertising, if a client had a particular problem with one of our account management team or with our creative people, I always found that the reasons for the problem were usually distorted and very one-sided. I learned that when you are able to sit with all parties, you are able to provide a balanced view and the issue is resolved successfully. On a number of occasions, both in my advertising days and at Gloria Jean's Coffees, when someone complained about an issue or a person, I learned very quickly to check the facts with all parties involved. A small number of franchisees in any industry will tell you that no one helps them, particularly the Master Franchisor. However, when you check it out, you will always discover that the franchisee has presented a blinkered view; the franchisee has exaggerated the misinformation and magnified his or her view out of proportion. It is always important to be able to sit with the individual and work through the facts. Certainly the Master Franchisee is not perfect, but when both parties develop a positive approach, this leads to a more balanced view and this helps them to get back on track far more quickly.

5) *Negativity will make sweeping statements and unfair judgments*

People who are in a negative state of mind will usually exaggerate the situation. They will often declare, "Everyone says this won't work!" or "Everyone thinks we should give up!" There have been many occasions when people have come to me and made similar statements such as, "Everyone is doing it this way." But when you ask who *everyone* includes, almost always you'll find that *everyone* ends up being one or two people. So in response to these sweeping statements, I learned to ask the question, "Who is everyone?" It's actually never everyone.

When I was in advertising, clients would say to me, "Everyone advertises in this publication, so book advertising for us in that publication too." But when I opened the publication, I discovered that everyone *didn't* advertise in it. It is easy to judge or criticize based on limited information. We are always forming our view or our opinions based on information given to us. That's why it is very important to explore as much information as possible so a better opinion can be formed or a better decision can be made.

Too many unfair judgments have been made through ignorance. Have all the information in front of you before you pass judgment on a situation or on someone. After all, that's what you would want others to do to you.

6) *Negativity limits the present and sabotages the future*
Negativity stunts your growth. If you have a negative attitude, you will stop growing; you will stop making wise decisions and this will slow your progress. People with a negative mindset tend to believe that every decision they make will bring about a poor result. If you are like that, you need to fight those thoughts by reminding yourself of your successes. You need to remind yourself of what you have achieved to date and start to develop a more balanced, positive attitude. By maintaining a negative spirit, you limit your effectiveness in the present and you sabotage your future; you stop moving towards the resources that will eventually bring you success.

So you can see that viewing every situation from a negative point of view is not a great way to manage your business, run your life or maintain relationships with other people. It's so easy to be negative with other people, but we have to learn to be positive and to see the best in each situation. We have to get away from the ceiling mentality in which we believe we have reached the ceiling or the potential in our business or relationships. If you believe you have achieved all that you can ever achieve, then you must believe that there are no more opportunities for you, and that is *never* the case.

Every time I sit with people who are having difficulty with their business or in a relationship, as we begin to talk through the possibilities, they get excited again at the potential that still exists for growth. Unfortunately, seemingly insurmountable obstacles force so many people to stay where they are in business and in relationships. They justify staying where they are through their own negative thinking.

Negativity leads to compromise in so many areas. A negative mindset will compromise to get the job done. A negative attitude will compromise the way you deal with others. For instance, I have found that if you compromise to keep someone in your business, you will end up losing them anyway. Compromise can also affect the way you manage conflict. When you face disagreement, never compromise in your negotiations. You need to be able to positively resolve situations without compromise. One way to do that is to learn to focus on those things with which everyone agrees. Then, when you are all on the same page, you can begin to discuss peripheral issues on other 'pages'. Often the things that aren't in agreement will end up getting resolved in an amicable way.

Compromise leads to 'average' in business and in relationships. If you begin to compromise, you fall into the trap of producing average results. You will find that you won't stand for anything worth fighting for. There won't be anything remarkable in your business or relationships. Compromise is for the weak, so be strong!

In the early 1900s, some farmers in Alabama, USA, could have been excused for being very negative. When the Mexican boll weevil devastated cotton crops throughout Alabama, farmers reverted to planting peanuts and ended up producing and harvesting more peanuts than any other county in the USA. Consequently, the town of Rucker erected a monument to mark the turning point at which prosperity smiled on them. The monument bore this inscription: "In profound appreciation of the boll weevil and what it has done as the herald of prosperity." These farmers could have easily developed a negative attitude and built a whole disaster strategy around that attitude. They could have been excused for embracing a victim mentality. Instead, with a positive attitude, this disaster was turned into a positive outcome. They planted a different crop which ended up becoming more profitable than cotton and which gave them a whole different way of life.

It's actually easy to be negative. After all, many of our friends, business associates and the media continue to look at life from a negative point of view. It is pervasive. It's all around us. So it is very hard to resist negativity. Yet those who do are well rewarded. So take a stand now. Look on the bright side. You have a great future ahead of you. Practice looking positively at all situations. It may be difficult, but always look for one good aspect in every situation, because that one good thing will encourage you to move on to the next stage. It will push you towards a better future.

Determine from this point on that every time you are down and your thought processes take a negative turn — every time you find yourself thinking the worst in any given situation — prompt yourself to declare, *What have I learned today? What good thing has happened to me today?* This will begin the process of boosting a more consistently positive attitude to life. Cast off negativity from your business and personal life and you will see your life achieve so much more!

take action | NOW!

one: Deal swiftly with negative thoughts and attitudes before they become large and entrenched obstacles. Nip negativity in the bud before it establishes root in your mind.

two: When facing periods of challenge and growth, be extra wary of negative thoughts that will creep up on you.

three: Be careful of the words you speak when you are tired, down and defeated. During these times you will be tempted to be negative.

four: Do not allow negative circumstances to rule you. When facing a challenge, make a decision to react in the positive rather than the negative.

five: Find positive people—including people who have experienced success—and let them speak into your life to counter the negative attitudes.

six: Do not allow yourself and others around you to magnify problems beyond reality. Always have a balanced perspective in every situation you face.

seven: Gather all the information you can before passing judgment on a situation or on someone. Ignorance has led to too many unfair judgments.

eight: Maintain a healthy, positive attitude to give yourself every chance of reaching your goals. Do this by regularly reminding yourself of your successes.

fifteen |
HONESTY & INTEGRIT'

Always do the right thing

"To thine own self be true."
William Shakespeare

"Truthfulness is the main element of character."
Brian Tracy

I once saw an old car sticker that declared, "Live so the preacher won't have to lie at your funeral." What are you like when no one else is around? *That* is the true measure of your integrity. Living a life of integrity is about doing the right thing... at home, at work, on the sports field, at the shops, and even when you are alone.

Values considered essential to an ethical life include: honesty, integrity, promise-keeping, fairness, caring for others, respect for others and accountability. I'm not saying we are all perfect in everything we do and say—far from it! But if your staff can't trust you and if your family can't trust you, then your integrity needs a lift.

Integrity is when our words and our actions line up. English historian and politician Thomas B. Macaulay said, "The measure on a man's real character is what he would do if he knew he would never be found out." South African preacher Pastor Ray McCauley once stated, "Image is what people think we are. Integrity is what we really are."

Integrity cannot exist without honesty; they must go hand-in-hand in our daily lives. Pastor McCauley once told a funny story about integrity and honesty. Two old ladies were walking through the grounds of an English country church and came upon a tombstone. The inscription read, "Here lies Joe Soap — a politician and an honest man."

"Good heavens!" said one lady to the other. "Isn't it awful that they put two people into the same grave!"

In business and in our personal relationships, we cannot be two-faced. We need to be consistent in all our dealings. If we are not, our staff, our business associates and our family will not know where they stand with us. If we are wonderful at home but not at work, the people around us will be confused and will find it difficult to trust us. Whether through the pressure of work or the desire to be taken seriously in the office, I have seen some people resort to dishonest and unethical behaviour to get what they want at work. And yet those same people may be angels at home! If we're not the same person at home and at work, then our staff do not know who we are or how we will react to any given situation. This leads them to lack confidence in us. We show no leadership when we are two-faced.

Conversely, if we are great with people at the office but terrible at home, our own children and our own partner will never know how to relate to us. They'll always be on edge around us. Solid relationships cannot be built that way. Is your nature and attitude the same whether you are at home, at work, on the sporting team, or when you go to church on Sunday? Do you have a consistent character? If not, then you need to change — for your own sake and for the sake of your family and friends.

When I was a director and heading up the media department at DDB Needham Advertising in the 1970s and 1980s I had many experiences with people in the advertising and media industries who could not be taken at their word. I was never a drinker, although the industry was renowned for its alcohol consumption. As I mentioned earlier in the book, on one occasion I was told by a fellow director that he could not trust anyone who did not drink! *Why?* I wondered. Then he informed me that he would not remember what he may have told me the night before, but that I *would* remember! He may have felt that with me around his tangled web might unravel and the lies would be revealed.

Be consistent and up-front in your dealings with your suppliers, your staff and your family. In this way, you are not trying to make up for things you have said to someone, and you are not attempting to negotiate your way out of a tangled mess of cover-ups and half-truths.

God, family and work

Ray Kroc of McDonald's fame once stated, "I believe in God, family, and McDonald's. And in the office, that order is reversed." I don't believe this should be the case. I don't even believe these should be priority-listed. When you prioritize your life in that way, you are simply creating conflict within yourself. Try to involve your family in your work, and your work in your family. Interlink each area of your life so that they don't all exist as completely separate parts. You can better balance your life that way.

I believe God wants to be part of our *whole* life — equally: our family, our work, our friendships, our church commitments, our sports involvement, and so on. He wants to influence every part of our involvement in life and not be tied down to *our* order of priorities. Every element of our lives is equally important to Him. So get rid of the priority list. In this way one element does not conflict with the other. Our lives come into better perspective when we see it from this viewpoint. When you put a priority on each of the parts of your life, then your work life may fight with your home life, and your church life may fight with your sporting life. Our lifestyle shouldn't be like that. We shouldn't be pulled from one aspect of our life to another. Treat each part with equal care and attention.

Keep your word

In days gone by, when people gave you their word and you

shook their hand, it was better than a signed contract. It was, in fact, seen as a covenant. How reliable is *your* word? Is your word your covenant? When you promise something, do you intend to deliver on it? If you don't, then you have an integrity problem.

I was responsible for a variety of clients in my advertising days, and there were times when I or my agency found we could not deliver on a commitment or we did not have the answer by the date promised. When that occurred, I made sure I called the client to keep them up-to-date with the situation. And generally there was no problem with the new commitment or the new arrangement. By keeping my clients informed of the problem, I developed great ongoing relationships.

The same communication issue has also come up within Gloria Jean's Coffees. On occasions, people left themselves open to accusations of dishonesty and distrust simply because they did not respond to phone calls or emails. I have discovered that people quickly lose faith in you, not necessarily because you fail to deliver exactly on time, but because you fail to communicate — whether to cover up mistakes or simply to avoid possible confrontation. In almost every case, the problem was resolved once regular and honest updates were given.

Don't be afraid to ring and let people know if there is a problem. If for some good reason you find that you are not going to be able to deliver on your word, rather than ignoring the person to whom you gave your word, you should go back to that person and apologise; then work out a way forward. In situations like that I have found people appreciate your honesty and openness and will work with you through the problem. However, your integrity is called to question when you hide the problem or try to paint over it. Don't be the type of person who gives their word to get a deal approved or to get a job done or to keep an employee... but doesn't have any intention of delivering on that promise. For the most part people will appreciate your honesty. In a world without much honesty and integrity, your open and honest actions will stand out like a beacon.

I believe we should keep our word at all times, even when we know it will cost us something. In 1942, as war threatened the Pacific, General Douglas MacArthur had to leave his base in the Philippines, and so he delivered those famous words, "I shall return!" In a speech in Australia nine days later the 62-year-old statesman reaffirmed his promise, saying, "I shall return!" Two years later, when he returned to the Philippines, he announced, "I have returned!" Despite overwhelming odds, the old soldier kept his promise. That kind of integrity is hard to find these days.

The Second Book of Timothy in the New Testament states that men are truth breakers, that they will tend to break their promises. Nowadays we question the promises of politicians, business can no longer be conducted on a handshake, and parents have good reason to doubt their children. King Solomon said, "It is better not to vow than to make a vow and not fulfil it." (Ecclesiastes 5:5)

Admit your mistake

So how about you? Do you keep your word, even when it costs you? When you say you will be somewhere on time, are you? When you tell people they can depend on you, can they? When you agree to pay your financial obligations on time, do you? Granted, nobody's perfect. But when you fail, do you admit your mistake without making excuses?

The old saying, "Be sure your sin will find you out", still rings true today. Hiding your problems will only postpone the inevitable. But revealing your mistakes — despite some possible short-term disapproval — will in the long-term attract support for your honesty and uphold your integrity. A wise man once said, "A good name is more desirable than great riches." (Proverbs 22:1)

Integrity is something we build up over time. We need to focus on consistently building a platform of good habits. When it comes to your values and your habits, you will discover that:

1. Some are good and just need to be reaffirmed
2. Some are inconsistent and need to be reinforced

3. Some are underdeveloped and need to be refined
4. Some are harmful and need to be repented of.

The bottom line is this: You will grow in stature if you commit yourself to being a person of outstanding integrity and honesty. Your employees, business associates, friends, family and supplier partners will look up to you. To have their trust and confidence is a thing of value. So commit to living a life of integrity and honesty. Then your staff won't have to guess which one of you has turned up for a meeting! And your family won't have to wonder which one of you has arrived for dinner!

take action |
NOW!

one: Avoid dishonest and unethical behaviour both at home *and* at work. Ignore this principle and your family members and work colleagues will find it hard to trust you.

two: Be honest and up-front in your dealings with your suppliers, your staff and your family.

three: Determine today to make sure you always keep your word — at home and at the office. And if there are times when you find you can't, then apologise, let them know you can't, and give them your 'Plan B'.

four: Involve your family in your work and your work in your family. Interlink each area of your life so that they don't all exist as completely separate parts.

five: Recognise that integrity is built up over time, so focus on consistently building a platform of good habits.

sixteen |

FAMILY

"None but a mule denies his family."
Arabian Proverb

The former French First Lady Yvonne de Gaulle once said, "Even the presidency is temporary, but family is permanent!" Many business people do not realise the importance of their family in their business. The truth is that your family will either support you and help get you to your vision, or your family will hinder you along the journey. Either way, it's up to you.

If your children end up going off the rails because you didn't spend enough time with them, it's going to be too late to say, "I wish I'd done it differently!" When I worked in the advertising industry, I saw many of my colleagues' relationships break down. They simply didn't pay enough attention to their family life. The hours in the advertising industry were — and still are — very irregular. We would never finish the working day at 5:00 pm; it was more likely to be 7:30 pm or later on a regular basis. And when my colleagues finished work, they would head straight to the bars or pubs and spend some time there before heading home. I was always conscious of going straight home so that I could spend time with my family.

Even when you arrive home, *how* you spend your time with your family is important. As business people, we often carry emotional baggage home with us. If we've had a bad day, it affects us mentally and emotionally. Sometimes things don't go according to plan at work. But here's my warning: Don't take it home with you! If something needs to be dealt with at work, then address it straight away. The apostle Paul said in the New Testament, "Do not let the sun go down on your anger." (Ephesians 4:26) There's wisdom in that.

If you spend all your life at work and don't invest in your relationships at home, then you will have problems at home. Relationship challenges at home will impact on your thought processes throughout your working day and this will have an impact on your business. Again, address it straight away so that you can focus clearly at work.

Leave your work at work

Your to-do list at work will always be there. You have to come to the realization that you will never get to the end of it. So at the end of each working day, leave it all behind you as you close the office or shop door. You are going to need to learn how to prioritise your work so that you are able to leave work at a reasonable hour to be able to spend time with your family. You need to constantly remind yourself that at work you cannot deal with everyone. You cannot solve everyone's problems. You might want to, but you are not able to do that. Once you come to terms with that, move on… and begin to get the priority jobs done in realistic timeframes.

Former CEO of General Electric, Jack Welch, once stated, "If you've been in your position for a year or more and must work 80-hour work weeks, you're doing something terribly wrong. Put down a list of 20 things you're doing that make you work that type of schedule and ten of them have to be nonsense." Put Jack's advice to work now. Write a list and then draw lines through some of the unimportant items.

King Solomon in the Old Testament talked about little foxes that ruin the vineyards. Small foxes seem harmless enough, but they dig holes that disrupt the soil around the plants, stopping the plants from developing a strong root system. It's the seemingly small and innocent things that end up undermining our relationships. These little foxes are like that one more hour at work—if it's repeated over and over it becomes disruptive to family time.

Today we work longer hours, resulting in neglected marriages and stressed-out partners. And it's not just men. The majority of working mothers today are still responsible for managing the home as well as their jobs. And let's not forget those stay-at-home mums who log 16-hour days with children demanding their attention.

Unfortunately, relationships suffer in both small and large businesses. This need not be the case. In small business particularly, the pressure can become intense. I have seen relationships suffer amongst franchisees across many franchise systems because they didn't share the journey with their partner. The pressure valve releases the moment they get home. During my working life, I have been guilty of this too. Today I recognise the symptoms a little quicker. Make a decision to change today and deal with this issue.

I once encouraged a franchisee to sell his store after we realised he could not address the pressure affecting his family. (While we want all our franchisees to have a successful business, we do not want the pressure to ruin family life.) After some time, he did sell and was able to restore relationships with his wife and children. For some, the answer lies in staff training and motivation so that hours of work are better managed. For others, it will mean learning to delegate responsibility. It's all about working *on* the business, not just *in* it.

Balance family and work

Some business people believe that family and business should be kept separate. However, as I mentioned in the previous chapter, I don't see how they can be detached. You live and breathe both, especially if you operate your own business. (I should note here that even as an employee I treated the business as my own, and you should do the same if you are in that situation.) You've got to learn how to balance both family and business so that they both become a part of your life. Learn to share the experiences of work with your wife or your husband in a positive way. The same goes for your children. Don't let the only time you share work with your family be when things are not going well. No one wants to hear complaints all the time. Too much negativity about the business will eventually shut you out. Share the positive aspects of your work. Make sure you talk about the fun things and celebrate the successes. Then your spouse will be more open to hear about your challenges at work and offer support during times of stress.

A common question people ask me is: How do you separate business and family life? To be frank, I don't believe they can be totally separated, especially if the business is one you own or run yourself and it plays a part in your dreams and aspirations in life. When you have successfully engaged your family in the process and they no longer see the business as a competitor of your time with them, there should be no real conflict. If you constantly cause them to feel neglected, they will not embrace the vision with you. And then who will they blame? Certainly not the business!

If we want to invest in a healthy relationship at home, we must watch our attitudes. Whether we like it or not, our spouse and our children catch our attitudes very easily. If our attitudes are positive, then we have nothing to be concerned about. But if we have some negative attitudes, they will affect our family.

During a leadership seminar on attitudes, a man once told author John Maxwell the following story:

From my earliest recollections, I do not remember a compliment from my father. His father also thought it unmanly to express affection or even appreciation. My grandfather was a perfectionist who worked hard and expected everyone else to do the same without any encouragement. And since he was neither positive nor relational he had a constant turnover in his employees.

Because of my background it has been very difficult for me to nurture or encourage my family. This critical and negative attitude has hindered me in life. I've raised five children and tried to live as a Christian before them. Sadly, it's easier for them to recognize my love for God than my love for them. They're starved for affection and approval. The tragedy is, they've received my bad attitude trait, and now I see them passing it down to my precious grandchildren.

Never before have I been so aware of 'catching an attitude'. Obviously, this wrong attitude has been passed along for five generations. So it's time to stop it!

Today I make a conscious decision to change. This will not be done overnight, but it will be done. It will not be accomplished easily, but by God's grace it will be accomplished.

You need to decide today if there are some attitudes you have that need to stop with you. If you can make these changes now, your children and your grandchildren will also be the beneficiaries. We need to make that change. We need to make that cut. It is time to draw a line in the sand. We need to influence and affect the next generations, otherwise it will continue.

No business person on their death bed ever said, "I wish I'd spent more time at work!" Learn to bring your family on your journey. You need to plan and enjoy family time. Share the vision with them. Share the successes. They are your most loyal supporters and they are the ones who will always cheer from the sidelines. This means also learning to relax at home. Leave your to-do list at work. Leave your business stresses at the office or the store.

Delegate to maximize your time

If you continually try to handle everything yourself and neglect to delegate responsibilities to other people, you will be constantly tired and your relationships at home will be impacted. Learn to pace yourself. Don't try to do everything or you will kill yourself, your business and your family.

We all multitask today to the point that we never focus clearly on any one thing. If you don't take time to see the big picture, you'll get lost in the details. Ask yourself, *What is it that only I can do?* Then give yourself to those tasks that only you can do and delegate the rest… or drop them. Multitasking is valuable and often needed in a new business that is starting out, but as soon as you can you must learn to start focusing and set priorities. Start delegating some of the responsibility to others - let others around you do it.

When we are anxious about our goals, we are not being fuelled by them. Instead, we are being stressed by them. You can't be a great visionary and at the same time be out of balance and end up neglecting what's important. Start to manage your time or others will. In order to be ready for the future, you must learn to pace yourself. The results will be that you will be able to provide leadership and innovation; you will be able to encourage and build your people; and you will be able to reap the rewards. Failure to do this will cause you to ruin great opportunities because you underestimated what it would take to get you to your destination.

Take care of yourself

Do you take work home? Do you stay up late after the children go to bed and your partner is asleep? Do you skip meals to catch up on paperwork, even though it keeps replenishing itself like weeds along a hillside? Do you drive to meetings while checking your electronic diary, drinking coffee and talking on the mobile phone? Isn't it crazy to run a portable office while driving at 100 kilometres an hour down the highway?!

Do you drive like the speed limits are just suggestions? Speed limits actually exist for a reason: our protection. Ignore them and you will one day crash! (At high speed the picture isn't pretty; survival rates are low) The same is true about life. Slow down to read the warning signs and avoid a catastrophe down the track.

A chaotic business life normally means that we are overlooking the basics, like food, sleep, exercise and, for many, time with God. Some of us take better care of our dogs and cats than we do of ourselves. Too often we view sleep and exercise as luxuries rather than necessities. Yes, there are occasions when we need to work late or put in an all-nighter, but this must not become a lifestyle. If you want to reach your destiny, your vision and your plan, you must organise your life accordingly and learn to pace yourself.

We all need to recognize that some seasons are busier than others. Occasionally, opportunities will come along that require extra time and attention, but you can't expect yourself to always travel at warp speed. You may feel that you are superman or superwoman right now, but sooner or later you will realize that you are mortal and fragile, and that your make-up is both physical and emotional. You are not a robot, a computer or an engine than can be operated at the flick of a switch. Even mechanical devices will fail or break down if you don't keep them fuelled and maintained.

Your spouse is also mortal and fragile, with both physical and emotional needs. So are your children. So invest in them and meet their needs. Learn to constantly express your appreciation at home. For instance, take your spouse on regular dates. Learn to look after her (or him). I once saw a list of the top ten car bumper stickers, and here are the messages on two of them:

If at first you don't succeed, do it the way your wife told you to do it!

I still miss my ex-husband, but my aim is getting better!

Unfortunately, many of us have similar attitudes towards our partners. But I've learned to appreciate my wife who, from day one, has been supportive and encouraging. At times she's had to pull me back on track because I've come home stressed-out or discouraged over events that have happened during the day.

Schedule time for relaxation

When Sue and I began the Gloria Jean's Coffees journey, things were not easy. There was no spare cash or investment capital we could tap into. Back then, in order to get the company going we both put in long hours, learning as we went along. Most days we would arrive home late and tired with no time to cook a meal. We had just enough energy to do the basic chores, fall asleep and do it all over again the next day.

We soon decided that we needed to *make* time for each other away from the business environment, and that meant turning off the mobile phones and relaxing. Expensive options were out of the question, so we took time to go for walks on the weekends. Sometimes we trekked through local bushland. At other times we caught a ferry around the city and discovered little-known harbourside trails. During these inexpensive travels we were able to talk without being interrupted. We were able to think more clearly, take in the scenery, and enjoy each other's company. Whatever relaxation option works for you, make sure you *make* time to do it. Schedule it into your diary. Turn off the mobile phone and pager. Do something simple that your family or your partner enjoys. Just spend time together.

Isn't it ironic that we used to take holidays to escape work, and yet today we take work with us on holidays via mobile phones, pagers and laptops. All that outside connection leaves us disconnected from each other.

The Old Testament tells us that children are a gift from God, but they still demand lots of our energy and time. I once read a statement from a woman who said, "I am with the children all day and by bedtime I'm exhausted. Then my husband wonders why I am not interested in intimacy. The last thing I need is another person pulling on me." Does that sound familiar to you? Well, learn to recognise the little foxes that destroy relationships by adopting some of these actions:

- Schedule regular dates together
- Turn off the TV and unplug the phone. (You'll be amazed at the difference that makes.)
- Hire a babysitter to take the children so you can spend time alone together.
- Take the weekend off with your family and do some fun things together.

take action |
NOW!

one: Begin to pay more attention to your family. Spend regular time with your partner and your children.

two: Don't take your business frustrations home with you. Don't infiltrate your home with negative attitudes from work.

three: Leave your work at work. Structure your work time so you get the priority jobs done in realistic time-frames and so you can get home to invest time in your family.

four: Learn how to balance both family and business so that they both become a part of your life. Learn to share the experiences of work with your wife or your husband in a positive way. Make sure you talk to your partner and children about the fun things and celebrate the successes. Share the vision with them.

five: Learn to delegate at work and start to pace yourself. Don't try to do everything or your busyness will harm yourself, your business and your family.

six: Schedule time for the basics, like food, sleep, exercise, relationships and, for many, time with God.

seventeen |

PARTNERSHIPS

"If we are together nothing is impossible. If we are divided all will fail."
Sir Winston Churchill

If you need money to start a business or to grow a business and you think acquiring a partner could be the solution, don't do it! A business partnership based purely on money will not succeed. For a partnership to be successful, you will need to be involved with people who share the same vision, the same passion, and the same commitment. You will need to be prepared to share openly about what is bugging you, about the direction of the business, and about decisions that need to be made. You will also need to agree on how to address disagreements, resolve issues and continue to move forward.

In franchising or in any other business in which people have formed a partnership because they needed money — whether it's a family member, a friend or a business associate — I do not know of any in which a disagreement has not occurred. Often what happens in this type of partnership is that someone will be a silent partner, someone will do the back-room work, and another party will do the front-end work, such as manage the retail store. In this situation, generally each party starts to believe the other person is lazy, isn't working hard enough, or isn't doing what they are supposed to be doing under the original agreement. This occurs especially when the business isn't performing to the expected levels. It also happens when the parties are not communicating and the problems become larger than life.

In a situation in which a partnership is involved in purchasing and running a franchise, unless you interview each of the parties and insist that each party goes through the training program, generally there will be disagreements about the implementation of that franchise. It's also important to ascertain where the money is coming from to purchase the business, because if each of the parties is stretched financially, this will cause tension in the partnership. For instance, one or both parties may struggle to pay back loans and this will disadvantage those who are involved financially, such as business partners or family members.

I have learned from my involvement with McDonald's and Gloria Jean's Coffees that when a husband or a wife wants to be a franchisee, you need to look at interviewing both partners, even if only one of them will be working in the business day-to-day. You need to establish if they are supportive of the business. If the husband or wife is not working in the business and is not totally supportive of their partner coming into the business, you will find that they end up with disagreements, relationships become strained, and they don't have a mutual understanding of the business. Generally the marriage either ends in divorce or there are disagreements that make life difficult for both parties.

McDonald's was always committed to interviewing all members of the family to make sure everyone understood what it meant to be in business and what it meant to be a McDonald's franchisee. This is important for all parties, for their ongoing health and their future together.

Co-branding partnerships

Another form of partnership is co-branding. This type of partnership occurs when two companies get together and share the same retail premises, or they share systems or business opportunities. Again, in going into a partnership of this nature, it is important to establish the parameters and how issues will be resolved, otherwise it will end up with the same problems as failed single-business partnerships.

At Gloria Jean's Coffees we have entered into a number of co-branding partnerships. In one instance, the original commitment and passion of the partnership was lost when there was constant staff turnover. Also, the standards could not be maintained and the passion was not embraced by the new management. In another instance, the positioning of our outlet was not conducive to a coffee drinking environment and we are currently working through a revised concept and new location positioning to maximise the opportunity.

On the other hand, co-branding can be very powerful. We have a very good working relationship with Borders Books in Australia where our outlets are able to provide the full Gloria Jean's Coffees experience within the context of their bookstores. This relationship benefits both Borders Books and our own stores.

The power of agreement

In the Old Testament King Solomon talked about the power of agreement. He said, "Two are better than one, because they have a good return for their work… A cord of three strands is not quickly broken." (Ecclesiastes 4:9, 12) The extra strands provide greater strength. With the right partnership you can have a powerful combination if you stand side by side, committed to each other, committed to the business, agreeing to meet, and agreeing to resolve the issues. There is great strength in partnership when done for the right reason, the right motivation, the right heart, and with real determination to succeed through the tough times.

The apostle Paul warned us in the New Testament about the combination of light and darkness. He said that as soon as light comes, the darkness goes. In the same way, a partnership of people who don't share the same vision, the same values, the same faith and the same commitment will not work. Instead, one party will dominate the other party. If you are in a business and your spouse doesn't work in that business, take care not to ignore your life partner. Your spouse is your best asset. Your spouse can be your best encourager. So learn to invest in them. (See the chapter on Family for more advice in this area.)

If a husband and wife are in business together, they must not forget to sow into that relationship away from the business. Even when they are tired, they have to commit to a short break away from anything to do with business. This helps to bring balance to the relationship.

Another key principle to healthy partnerships is the ability to listen in full to every idea your partner shares with you. Never brush them off. Each one is an equal partner and deserves to be given equal consideration. As I have said before, two heads are better than one. I know of one couple who are in a partnership who said this: "We have sit-down sessions together after we get home. We will bring up whatever we want and, out of respect, we don't interrupt each other. We each take a turn to talk." That's great advice for any partnership, whether married or not, whether in business together or not.

Another issue that crops up is a partner who is not committed in the same way to the same vision, values and dream that you have. This kind of partner will try to cannibalise your dream. It's often someone who never embraced the dream for themselves in the first place. Over time the opposing partner will subtly try to sabotage your dream. They may not be blatantly in opposition, but they will tend to slowly erode your confidence by niggling away at you. This type of partner may be a family member, a relative or a friend.

Make sure your partner is on the same journey

When you have the dream, the vision and the passion, make sure your business partner and your life partner are on the same journey with you. And make sure they want to be a part of it. Learn to share with your partner. Encourage them to grow. Learn to share your dreams and refine these dreams together so that you are both able to embrace them without conflict.

While some partners may be very supportive of your dream, even confirming that yours is a *great* dream, in the end remember that it's *your* dream. Don't radically change it because of something they may want. Sometimes your dream will cause people to say,

"You've gotta be kidding!" Remember, that's just their opinion, not yours. And it's not *their* dream, it's *your* dream. While it may need some refining to come into being, it needs to remain essentially *your* passion.

Dreams separate winners from losers, and dreamers who actually do the hard work to see their dreams realised are rare. Dreamers are always a minority. Those who walk by sight will always outnumber those who walk by faith. You need to believe and be committed to your dream. That's why you need a partner who shares the same passion and the same vision, someone who shares the same values.

Great partnerships are rare and highly valued. Most partnerships start off well with great intentions. But many business people have been burned by partnerships that turned sour. That's why there are hundreds of stories of partnership disasters. But don't be scared off by partnerships.

Dr Ern Crocker, a friend of mine, once shared with me that most people try to get out of deep water as fast as they can. But he said there are times when we need to embrace it. He offered this advice:

1. If you only step into the water up to your ankles, you will only get your feet wet.
2. If you wade in up to your knees, you may splash around a lot and get pretty wet… but you will only make slow progress.
3. If you try to battle on in your own strength at waist height, you will become even slower.
4. It's only when you are out of your depth that you will begin to see the real blessing. Why? Because only then will you stop doing things in your own strength. Out in the deep you will actually relax and float and swim. So stop standing on tippee toes to prevent yourself from drowning. Let go of the sand under your feet and start to swim and enjoy the water.

My friend was relating this experience to his relationship with God. He recognised that he needed to jump in, not just wade in.

In a partnership you need to realise that you can't just enter the water up to your ankles. In a partnership you are in at the deep end, so you've got to learn to swim and paddle. In a partnership, just wading into the water won't cut it.

Partners have different strengths

In a partnership you've got to support each other, because that is where the blessing and success will unfold. Partnerships are all about sharing the workload, but partners must also recognise that different people have different strengths. In the Old Testament, Moses led the Israelites through the wilderness. He demonstrated that he was a political and diplomatic leader. He patiently listened to the people's many complaints. He led the people as a peacemaking shepherd and he provided water from a rock when the people got thirsty.

But Moses wasn't the person to take them into the Promised Land. The Israelites needed a different leader who could stand with them as they faced very fierce enemies. Joshua was appointed as leader. He was totally different to Moses. He led the people through 30 years of conquering Caanan. He was a military 'in-your-face' leader. He confronted laziness and the fear of the enemy. He led people as a tough commander. For instance, when the people complained about being thirsty he told them to dig their own wells!

We need to remember that there are different types of partnerships in which people can fulfil different roles at different times. Each one of us is unique, sometimes because we have different backgrounds, but a partnership can work by understanding our different qualities and by regularly sharing with each other.

Pastor Grant Thomson from Hillsong Church in Sydney once spoke about partnership at an event I attended. He said that one of the key principles of a successful partnership is to focus on the good things. It's always easy to focus on the negative qualities in people, but to achieve a healthy partnership we should instead look at people's positive qualities. Now, that does not mean you shouldn't talk about matters that need addressing. It simply means that it's easy for us to focus the majority of our time on the bad things. He also spoke about focussing on things that don't divide. In the world today, it's unfortunate that people want to focus on things that will separate rather than on things that will unite.

We're on the same side!

Through my many years in advertising and at Gloria Jean's Coffees, there have been times when I've had to say to people on our staff or in business with us, "You need to understand that we're on the same side!" When we are working with people, whether in a partnership or in a work environment, sometimes we have to remind our people that we're all on the same side. We're all in the same business. We've all got the same vision, mission, goals and values. Sometimes we won't get that team feeling in the way that we all relate to one another. But in these situations we need to learn to pursue peace, not separation.

The *Sydney Morning Herald* in Australia published a story in its Enterprise section on 18 April 2007 that caught my interest. It talked about husband and wife teams who operated very successfully in business. In the article a couple called Stephen and Janine Harvey shared what they called their 'Peace Plan'.

They listed seven tips for couples in small business:
1. Consider the skills you each have — are they complementary?
2. List all the tasks needed to run your business
3. Divide the tasks evenly
4. Allow your partner some autonomy
5. Talk about what you are doing at work
6. Agree on a daily cut-off from 'shop talk'
7. Ensure you have time off together.

The same article also told the story of Trish Forsyth and her husband, Andrew. They had once shared a business in Sydney, but had eventually moved to the Daintree in Far North Queensland where they each had separate jobs. They said the biggest difference between sharing a business with your partner and working alone is the need to share responsibilities. On your own, you are used to having total control over what everyone is doing. But with a partner, you need to split responsibilities down the middle.

If you find a good *partner*, then you have found a very good thing. If you find the right partner, be certain you've found one of life's greatest gifts. But, be warned, if you choose the wrong partner the results can be devastating. In a business partnership, as in a marriage relationship, you will need to work at it—constantly communicating and confronting issues together, never taking the relationship for granted.

When difficulties arise

All partnerships, whether in business or otherwise, require work in order to remain healthy. They will not flourish when there is no communication, when things are allowed to drift or when either person feels left out or neglected. If you are in this situation, make a decision now to re-establish some ground rules. See 'Take Action Now!' below for my list of suggestions.

take action |
NOW!

one: If your husband or wife is in business with you, remember to sow into that relationship by regularly committing to short breaks away from anything to do with business.

two: Pay attention to every idea your partner shares with you.

three: Make sure your business partner and your life partner are on the same journey with you; who are equally committed to the same vision, values and dream that you have.

four: If you are in a partnership with someone right now, understand each of your different qualities and regularly share with each other.

five: To achieve a successful partnership, you will need to focus on the good qualities of your partner.

six: If you are experiencing challenges in your partnership, learn to pursue peace, not separation. After all, you are both on the same team!

seven: If your partnership is not flourishing, make a decision now to re-establish the ground rules—here is my list:
- Make regular meeting times and stick to them
- Communicate openly and honestly
- Re-look at the vision, mission and values you established for the business and evaluate where you are in relation to these
- Come to agreed plans of action and write them down
- Be an encouragement… stick to the positive without ignoring the challenges
- If you decide to exit, work out how you can do that in a planned, positive way.

eighteen |

GET A COACH

"Two are better than one, because they have a good return for their work."
Ecclesiastes 4:9

I have a friend with a similar sense of humour and positive outlook on life whom I meet on a regular basis for lunch, ten pin bowling or snooker. We meet once a week if possible. When we get together we are able to relax and share about various aspects of business.

It's important to have someone with whom you can regularly meet so that you can share thoughts and ideas. I have met with another loyal and supportive friend for some 16 to 17 years every Wednesday morning at 6:30 am — except when one of us is away. We take that time to meet together, share with each other, discuss and pray about our businesses, talk about our families, support and encourage one another and share ideas.

Meeting regularly with friends like this is important so that you get things off your chest. A good friend you can trust to keep things in confidence and one who can trust you to do the same is invaluable. These are the people who stick by you in times of crisis, who don't pull you down when you've made mistakes. These are special people who encourage you and whom you respect enough to heed their advice.

These friendships are valuable. If you are facing a challenge in business or in a relationship, your friend can offer you sound advice because he (or she) knows you well. Your friend isn't caught up in the difficult situation and can therefore offer you objective advice. You can also talk about some great ideas or solutions to problems, and often your friend may be able to offer you names of contacts who would be helpful in developing your ideas. You may not necessarily discuss major problems or solutions every week, but you will certainly benefit from having someone with whom you can share your experiences and thoughts.

If Tiger Woods — the greatest golfer in the world — needs a coach, who says you don't need one! By 'coach' I mean find someone who is going to be positive, someone who is going to be able to sow into your life. Find someone who doesn't think with 'bottom of the pile' mentality. They don't need to be qualified or professional 'coaches'. They could simply be someone who is successful in life and a good friend who can give you different viewpoints. Remember, this relationship goes both ways; you will drain the relationship dry if input and encouragement is all one way. Friendships should always be mutually beneficial.

There are two ways to approach the concept of a 'coach':
1. Someone you regularly meet with to share and encourage one other.
2. Someone you seek advice from in a specific way, a person who has been where you want to go. This coach relationship may be either long-term or short-term. And this type of coach may be someone you only see when the opportunity arises or it may be on-going over many years.

Both types of coach relationships are vital in your life if you want to progress. The principles I want to present to you will apply both to a short-term and a long-term coaching relationship.

Find someone you can trust

If you are the owner or the managing director of a business, there are probably few people within your business with whom you can share the difficulties you face. Having another person to share with will encourage you in your role. Having someone you trust and who you can confide in will enable you to be able to deal with difficult situations much better than if you had to face these situations alone. The right 'coach' can encourage you with wise advice and with much-needed encouragement. As they say, two heads are better than one because there are two minds on the problem.

Remember not only to find a coach, but to become a coach. One thing I have discovered in life is that when you start giving in an area where you need input, you gain or attract that very thing into your own life. For example, if you start becoming an encouragement to other people, you will attract positive encouragement from others. If you are a good and faithful friend and confidant, others will become that to you. The Bible talks about the law of sowing and reaping. It says that whatever you sow in life you will reap. (Galatians 6:7-10) If you sow fun into someone, you will attract fun from others. If you sow kindness into someone, you will reap kindness, and so on.

Things to Avoid

In seeking to build a coach relationship, there are some guidelines to follow to ensure the relationship remains healthy, effective and balanced. Here are some things to avoid. First, make sure you avoid manipulative relationships. Don't buy someone's friendship by letting them manipulate you. If you do, you will only keep on paying for it.

Second, don't plan on changing them to your way of thinking. The object is to learn, grow and support each other; it's not to change the other person into a reflection of you, having the same thoughts and opinions as yours. Author Betty Bender said, "It's a mistake to surround yourself only with people just like you."

Third, don't fear the other person or feel intimidated by them, especially if they have had more experience or achievements than you. And don't be fearful of advice or opinions which are confronting; you may need these from time to time. King Solomon said, "The fear of man is a dangerous trap." (Proverbs 29:25) Fourth, don't go against your values just to be more acceptable to the other person. Relationships don't survive with one person calling all the shots.

Fifth, when you share with each other, don't judge each other's opinions. Last, don't expect perfection. After all, we are all human and we all make mistakes. Always listen to suggestions, opinions, fears and ideas without dismissing or pre-judging them.

Things to commit to

Now, here are some things to commit to:
First, learn to listen to and serve each other. Listening with an open mind is the key. Don't listen just for your own gain, but listen with an attitude of commitment to the other person. Be genuinely interested in the other person.

Second, be honest with each other. No one can fully support, assist and encourage you if you hold back or are less than honest about what is going on in your life. This may mean that you need to deal with pride in your life. If so, then deal with it quickly so that your coach can help you progress.

The apostle Paul wrote, "I'm with you all the way, no matter what. I have… the greatest confidence in you." (2 Corinthians 7:5) Paul was the Corinthians' greatest cheerleader, despite their many faults and mistakes. He knew how to correct, comfort, encourage and sharpen them. He also was honest and straightforward with them about his own difficulties.

If you want to see growth in your own life and in your coach's life, then see your coach or mentor as more than a statistic. It's all about the relationship. Mary Kay Ash, founder of Mary Kay Cosmetics, said, "P&L doesn't mean profit and loss, it means people and love." I want to encourage you to see your business that way too: It is made of people and love. Your business is held together with relationships.

I have often visited store construction sites, and at the beginning they look nothing like the store they will become. In fact, in the week before opening there is nothing but a shell. There may be pipes, concrete plinths, holes in the walls and ceiling, and rubble everywhere. Some franchisees start to worry when they see the mess. *How will this ever come together?* they wonder. It isn't until the last two or three days that things begin to take shape: Cupboards, pastry cabinets, lighting, signage, tiles, floorboards and finally equipment is installed. Only when the hoardings come down and the furniture is arranged can you really appreciate the hard work that has been done.

It's the same when you and your coach begin to meet and share together. There will be constant construction work going on in both your lives. I have seen this with the men with whom I share a coaching relationship: Their lives go through stagnant periods and then move forwards... they grow and change. And they have seen the same in me. Only when you look at the progress and achievements made can you appreciate the time you took to build the relationship.

In going through these sharing times with a coach, don't get 'used up'. Keep learning yourself — don't depend on the coaching relationship to do it all for you. As you face each day with new deals and new obstacles, you will be able to bring greater value to the relationship as you share and reflect on these things. There is nothing worse than a situation in which you both stagnate or, worse, get drawn into a downward spiral.

Author Bob Gass once told a story in his daily devotional *The Word for Today* booklet about a woman waiting for a bus in a dangerous neighbourhood. A rookie cop asked her, "Do you want me to wait with you, Miss?"
"No thanks, I'm not afraid," she replied.
"Then," he grinned, "Would you mind waiting with me?"

You move from being a likely victim to being a victor by facing fears head on *with* your coach. Many business people feel they need to go it alone. They don't share with anyone and have no worthwhile input or encouragement in their lives. They relate to no one and, as a result, make poor managers.

"Don't assume that you know it all," said King Solomon in Proverbs 3:7. We're not always as smart as we think we are.

Often, sharing with a coach gives us a reality check.

During your working life there may be a number of coaches with whom you develop a relationship. Never feel that you are tied to the one person. You may have all the commitment and faithfulness in the world, but there may be times when you need to change. There will also be times when you need specific input and your current coach relationship will not be able to help you in that area. So don't allow one person to be your only source of encouragement.

Your spouse or partner as a coach

If you are in a relationship with a partner, don't forget that your partner can be your greatest source of encouragement. In other words, your partner can be your coach as well. From time to time most people get more 'advice' than they can handle from their partner. However, if you are committed to building a business together, then you need to set aside time specifically to encourage one other.

Sue and I have been working together in various ways now for some time. Prior to starting Gloria Jean's Coffees, my job in advertising was quite separate from Sue's work. We have always had a very strong marriage relationship, and it has only become stronger through the experiences we've had working together at Gloria Jean's Coffees. There is no doubt that, especially in a family business, working together as partners is intense. The focus can be all-consuming. We therefore found it essential to set aside time specifically to share and encourage one another in a positive way.

While the tendency is to be in constant dialogue about problems and issues, make sure you set aside time specifically to look at your goals and the progress being made. This will be quite apart from the day-to-day support you hopefully give each other and will help build positive day-to-day goals.

This time should be structured so that each of you can share objectively without personal issues and judgements entering in. As in any relationship, each person's input should be valued, not discounted, and there should be time for creative problem-solving. This time does not need to be long. Once you have your vision and direction established, half an hour will often be enough. It can even be over a dinner or a lunch date.

A word of caution here: Don't do it when either of you are tired or pressed for time. It is best to diarise this as a meeting so that there is no 'escape'. Bring along any positive input each of you have received and not yet shared. Note down ideas, changes to make, positive steps taken… and read them to each other next time you meet.

Another word of warning: Don't make this the only time you share! Take an opportunity each day to do little things for each other that are totally unrelated to work, such as a shoulder massage, a special treat, a note or an email of thanks. (It is amazing how little we do of this for our own partners!) Remember, your partner should be your biggest asset. So take the initiative and enjoy the incredible support he or she can be.

Too many people—especially in business—feel they are too busy for close relationships with others. They feel their business, their families and their hobbies or sports are pulling their lives apart at the seams. So how can they find the time to meet regularly with a close friend and coach?! Well, how can they afford not to? The right friendships will help bring peace to a busy schedule. The right coach will help to bring balance to a chaotic life. So start to develop those key relationships now.

take action |
NOW!

one: Find someone with whom you can regularly meet so that you can share thoughts and ideas.

two: Choose someone you can trust and who you can confide in.

three: Don't just find a coach, but become a coach as well.

four: Maintain healthy, effective and balanced mentoring relationships by:
- Making sure you avoid manipulative relationships.
- Don't change the other person into a reflection of you.
- Don't fear the other person or feel intimidated by them.
- Don't go against your values just to be more acceptable to the other person.
- Don't judge each other's opinions.
- Learn to listen to and serve each other.
- Be honest and up-front with each other.

nineteen |

SUPPORT YOUR COMMUNITY

The rewards of generosity

"We make a living by what we get, but we make a life by what we give."
Sir Winston Churchill

Have you ever heard the saying "It's more blessed to give than to receive"? That old-fashioned advice many mums give their kids is actually true! And the reason this is true is that there are great rewards for generosity. Let me prove it to you.

The Bible says, "Whoever sows sparingly will also reap sparingly, and whoever sows bountifully will also reap bountifully." (2 Corinthians 9:6) The Book of Proverbs in the Old Testament says, "The world of the generous gets larger and larger; the world of the stingy gets smaller and smaller." (Proverbs 11:24)

King Solomon, many say the richest man who ever lived, tells us in the Book of Ecclesiastes that he reached the stage at which he seemed to have everything. And yet something led him to finally ask, "What is life?" Despite his great wealth, he felt that there was still something missing. I believe he simply didn't have a reason beyond himself. I believe that if he had been able to see what he could do with his vast resources, his life would have embraced real purpose.

We should all enjoy the benefits of the journey we are on. The Book of Timothy in the New Testament says the hard working farmer must be first to partake of his crops. (2 Timothy 2:6) King

Solomon even said that people should eat and enjoy the fruit of their labour. (Ecclesiastes 5:18) When David went to fight Goliath, he did not shy away from the rewards the king offered him: the king's daughter, wealth and exemption from taxes for life. Three times he asked the king to confirm the rewards, so it was obviously important to him. But David knew there was a greater purpose and that was to go out and defeat the enemy. He did it for the greater good, for his community... and the king's rewards followed.

In the movie *Jerry Maguire*, Tom Cruise made famous the line, "Show me the money!" But it's not always about money. Don't misunderstand me; there is nothing wrong with enjoying the rewards of our hard work, such as owning homes, enjoying holidays and driving the best cars. But if it's only about *us*, then I believe that's a selfish attitude. I don't believe we are here just to enjoy the wealth we may have created. I truly believe we are here to succeed in business, in relationships, and in life... so that we can be a blessing to those in need. We are to succeed so that we can support others.

Therefore we should be looking for creative ways to help those in need, whether in our own nation, overseas or indeed both. The benefits we will receive will far outweigh the actual rewards. As an individual, you should be looking for opportunities to be able to share what you are earning with other people. And our businesses should be exploring the best ways to invest in those in need.

Build community support into your business

There are many ways that individuals and businesses can help people. Some examples are:
1. We can give products that schools, charities, sporting groups and church groups can use to raise money.
2. We can provide the opportunity for groups of school students who are studying business to visit our premises to learn about our business.
3. We can donate money to causes.

4. We can provide jobs. We can provide jobs to disadvantaged people. We can employ those who have experienced tough times and who have graduated from life-building programs (such as Teen Challenge or Mercy Ministries). During the years that Gloria Jean's Coffees ran a warehouse facility, we employed and trained several Teen Challenge graduates. Of these young men, most proved extremely loyal workers and two went on to start their own businesses.
5. We can give our staff opportunities to attend seminars or workshops for their personal growth and development. At Gloria Jean's Coffees we pay for all our female staff to attend an annual women's conference that enhances their personal growth and development. The conference runs over a Friday and Saturday, so we give them the day off on the Friday. That policy was fine in the early days when we only had one or two women. We now have significantly more! It means we can invest not only in their future, but in the business's future as well. We provide similar opportunities for our men.

When we commenced Gloria Jean's Coffees, our aim was to provide resources to help the community. And over the years we have been able to contribute our time, products and finances to many schools, charities, church groups and sporting groups. We are not in a position to be able to help everyone—we have obligations to paying bills and meeting banking requirements—but community support has been deliberately and strategically built into our business plan. Our community support comes from two areas: One from the company and the other from our stores.

Compassion

Let me give you an example of how this works. As a company, in January 2005 Gloria Jean's Coffees partnered with an organisation called Compassion International who team up with local communities to provide support programs for children at risk in poverty stricken areas of the world. Initially we sponsored 50 children in a village in a coffee growing region of Brazil. A month later this grew to 100 children. At our international conference in Hawaii in 2006, sponsorship by our franchise partners added another 32 children to the program. A few franchisees have taken on sponsorship of more children since then, and members of our staff have sponsored 15, so we now have a total of 300 children whom we have sponsored. These are disadvantaged children who are now, as part of the program, dressed, fed and educated. This program benefits the whole family, not just the children, and it also benefits the rest of the village.

We like the idea of focusing our support in one area. You may want to do it differently through your business, but when you support one village you see a group of families' lives changed, and eventually you will see a whole village changed. We hope one day to see a whole town changed, then a city changed, then a country changed.

A women's correctional centre

When the New South Wales Government approached us in 2004 to open a store inside the new women's correctional centre at Windsor, we instantly agreed. Afterwards, I thought, *What have we done!* We soon discovered that the women in this correctional centre usually have no hope for their future when they leave the centre because no one will employ them. This is despite the fact that when they are trained in a career, most of them never re-offend. Most of these women are also single parents with the primary responsibility of raising their children. The children regularly visit their mums in the centre.

Well, we opened a Gloria Jean's Coffees store in that correctional centre in 2005. Today, not only does the store operate in the visitor area, it also provides training for women inmates, as well as a safe, warm atmosphere for children to visit (because the visitors area is also equipped with a playground). Since this store has been running, we've already employed three women who have been released from the correctional centre. When we opened the store one young lady said to us, "Do you realise that I now believe I've got a future and a hope!" She now has the skills and confidence needed to gain a job when she is released.

Opportunity International

We also support Opportunity International through a donation of AUD$10,000 (approximately USD$8,500) into a Trust Bank. This funding provides low interest loans to enable people in third world countries to start small businesses. Many people in third world countries only need a small loan to buy a bicycle, a boat, a sewing machine or products to sell in roadside convenience stores. History shows evidence that almost all the loans are paid back!

Many of these microenterprises now employ people, have paid back their loans, and have borrowed again to grow to the next level. The truly exciting aspect of a microenterprise loan is that it can keep regenerating itself into new businesses. We were also able to work with Opportunity International during the 2004 Asian tsunami to run a short-term fundraising campaign through our stores. We were able to raise a significant amount of funds through the hundreds of cash donation boxes and promotions in each of our stores.

Mercy Ministries

However, our ongoing key focus is Mercy Ministries. This is a residential program for young women in crisis. Currently there are two Mercy Ministries homes in Australia – in Queensland and in New South Wales. There will be further homes opening around the country in 2007 and beyond. Internationally our stores will be able to help provide funds and awareness through the placement of cash donation boxes and leaflets about Mercy Ministries on store counters. This gives the charity credibility and awareness in the marketplace.

In October every year Gloria Jean's Coffees stores in Australia run the 'Cappuccino for a Cause' weekend during which 50 cents from every one of our Cappuccinos or Cappuccino Chillers is donated to Mercy Ministries in Australia. Because of the campaign's butterfly theme, we also sell butterfly-shaped chocolates through our stores. These and other related programs increase awareness for Mercy Ministries through public relations activities and commercials on radio and television. Each year our franchisees take the cause to heart, many of them decorating their stores with balloons and providing face painting, clowns and entertainment to raise funds for Mercy Ministries... and bring in more Cappuccino sales! We are looking to expand the 'Cappuccino for a Cause' fundraiser internationally as Gloria Jean's Coffees and Mercy Ministries expand around the world.

Choose the right charity partners

These initiatives endorse our values as a company. They show that as an organisation we have a heart, and when people see that heart they warm to it. Our customers are happy that the company is involved in helping other people in so many areas. In the same way, your own business can benefit from an alliance with the right charity or cause. My advice is to find charities or causes that will 'fit' with your business and allow you and your staff to link up positively with the charity or cause.

Look for a charity or cause you can partner with to provide them with exposure and credibility in the marketplace. The partnership has to be one you and your staff can really feel involved in. You need to look for something you have a passion for and a desire to support. Don't just take on any cause; meet with them and make sure they are accountable and have systems in place and a track record in achieving success.

At the back of this book I have listed some organisations that you could be involved in. There are many others I have not been able to list.

A warning to charities here: If you are an organisation that receives support from a business or an individual, do you honour your sponsors and supporters? Do you keep them up to date with your activities and your achievements? Do you meet with them to thank them? Do you encourage them to stay involved in your great cause? There are some charitable organisations that take the money and never acknowledge their supporters or keep them up to date.

On the other hand, there are charities that actively engage with their business supporters. These are charities that understand the benefits for both the business and the charity. Both parties know that there is a win-win for both of them.

Why sponsor a charity?

Community sponsorship will provide your company with an opportunity to demonstrate concern and give back to the community. Other benefits include:

1. It builds loyalty.
2. It creates positive media coverage.
3. You feel great that you are able to help people.
4. Your family gets excited by what your company is doing… and your involvement in it.
5. It builds overall trust and long-term credit for the company image.
6. It enables companies to publicly position themselves in helping to provide a solution to a community problem.
7. Staff appreciate their company supporting a cause outside themselves. Customers and clients also love it.
8. Experience proves that staff will get behind a company's commitment in raising funds and they will provide word-of-mouth support.
9. Employees share with relatives and friends about the great company they work for.
10. People are less critical of a company that gives to the community.
11. Many customers walk into a Gloria Jean's Coffees store to support the business that supports people.

One last word of advice on this topic: It is important that we invest in the lives of our youth. We need to remember that the next generation will produce the future leaders of government, business, media, community, church, education and the arts. It is therefore important that we contribute positively into the lives of the next generation. Who knows, your input may influence and shape the very future of your country!

take action |
NOW!

one: Look for creative ways to help those in need around you, or in another state, or overseas. This may be in the form of jobs, donations, raising awareness, offering expert advice or skills, and so on.

two: Look for opportunities to share what you are earning with others. Your business should explore the best ways to invest in those in need.

three: Form an alliance with the right charity or cause. Find charities or causes that 'fit' with your business.

twenty

FRANCHISING

The opportunity to own your own business

"Fran•chise From Anglo-French ... to free."
Merriam-Webster Dictionary

There are many ways to do business. One of them is franchising. I have been privileged to work with two of the most successful franchises in Australia: McDonald's and Gloria Jean's Coffees. In my advertising days I worked closely on the McDonald's account, helping to establish the McDonald's brand in Australia. I have seen so many Australians achieve their dreams through owning a McDonald's franchise.

When I first started working on the McDonald's account, there were only a few McDonald's restaurants in Australia. Today there are 730 restaurants and 70 percent of those are owned and operated by local business people. McDonald's has been successful because it has been focused. From day one in Australia, the company set the direction and led the way. Needless to say, this led to some challenges. For instance, franchisees were not always in agreement. I have learned that franchisees like this can easily become 'my store' focused. But you cannot allow this attitude to drag you down to their (store) level. Everyone in a franchise needs to work together to build the brand and then each store will benefit from the flow-on effect.

I know from experience that franchising can achieve far more for an individual than other business models. Sure, other business models can bring you success, but at a retail level it is very difficult to build a brand and deliver the experience. It comes down to customer service, friendliness, ambience and a relaxed atmosphere. This is often generated by your people or the buzz within the store… or the colours in the store, the lounges, and the tub chairs that give a relaxed and friendly feel. It also includes being able to name customers and being able to dialogue with them about things other than a cup of coffee.

I am an advocate for franchising in any country because there are so many plusses for the franchisees, for the local communities, and for the nation. I have seen franchising help to build the dreams of so many people. It provides opportunities for people to build business skills. It provides access for many to own their own business. As an industry sector, it provides substantial employment opportunities and creates great wealth for any nation. But franchising, like anything else, requires hard work, consistency, commitment and a willingness to learn and grow.

I believe the rapid success of franchising in Australia over the past five or so years has been brought about because the Federal Government introduced the Franchising Code of Conduct in 1998. I'm not normally a fan of a lot of government legislation, but this one piece of legislation brought credibility and accountability to the whole franchising sector. That's why a number of credible, successful franchise businesses in Australia have been on a powerful growth path.

Australia's AUD$128 billion (USD$109 billion) franchise industry is growing extremely fast. There are well over 960 franchises in Australia employing about 600,000 Australians. Franchising provides the equivalent of 14 percent of the national GDP in Australia. This equates to 50 percent of small business turnover in Australia, yet from only 5 percent of small business outlets. According to the Franchise Council of Australia, more than four out of five franchise businesses are still operating after five years. That's an 80 percent success rate in the first five years. The picture is quite different for the average small business in Australia. I understand the picture is nowhere near as positive for independent small businesses. The website of the Franchise Council of Australia states that only 20 percent of independent small businesses are still operating after the first five years. So franchising is a great industry to be in these days.

Now, I realize that there will always be underperforming operators in any business sector. Unfortunately, we have to accept that that is life. But franchising, if done correctly, can minimize a lot of these situations. For example, the franchisor (the owner of the business providing the product or service) can assist franchisees to lift their results with well implemented systems. By the same token, franchisees can also positively impact their franchisor and the whole brand by following the system, by building strong community connections, and by executing great marketing plans.

Finding the right owner-operator (a franchisee who doesn't just own the local franchise, but who also rolls up his or her sleeves to work in the business) is crucial to the success of a franchise. As a franchisor, if you can find the right franchisee who is an owner-operator, then that person will build a powerful franchise model for you. That person will be involved in the community and will see their business grow consistently, in spite of the level of competition in their respective market. The right owner-operator franchisee will be passionate and committed, because they have their own money on the line. They will provide excellent customer service, they will look after their staff, and they will maintain the standards needed to be part of the brand. The right franchisee will also avoid a victim mentality; a franchisee who thinks that everyone is out to get them won't adequately focus on the business and the business will suffer.

The benefits of franchising

By now you may have guessed that I'm a firm believer of franchising! There is a whole range of strengths to franchising, such as greater opportunity for success, local ownership, consistency of systems, marketing support at a local and national level, community support (building relationships with schools, churches, sporting clubs and charities), the opportunity for members of the franchise family to take care of each other, and the opportunity to focus on the business without all the additional matters of sourcing products and negotiating prices.

Franchising appeals to so many people because it provides opportunities for people to own their own business, particularly if they have been retrenched or their employer has gone out of business. Franchisees see that this is their own business and that they can take more control over their destiny. The franchising concept attracts young people with a passion to own their own business. It attracts older people who want to grow a business that their family can contribute to. And it appeals to those who have a passion to work in a chosen field while growing something of value for themselves.

The breadth of the franchise market today has expanded to allow people to work in a business with a product, a brand or a service that they actually like. Most people work because it is a means to paying the bills. A seek.com.au survey in 2006 found that 37 percent of Australians hate their job. In his book *Cure for the Common Life, New York Times* bestselling author Max Lucado stated that one-third of Americans also hate their job.

For people who don't enjoy their work, franchising offers tremendous hope because it offers so many opportunities for them to choose a business environment that they enjoy. These days, the range of franchises offers people the choice to work indoors or outdoors, with customers or in the back office, serving food and drinks or handling animals, helping young people become home owners or helping seniors retire financially free. Franchising gives so many people a wonderful opportunity to have fun while earning a living.

Misunderstandings and problems in franchising

Despite all these benefits, some people are still skeptical of franchising. Unfortunately, many people still don't fully understand franchising. And this misunderstanding exists not just amongst friends and family, but also in professional industries such as law, accounting and the media. People can be critical of a successful business model through simple ignorance of the way the industry operates. On the other hand, there are also many supporters of franchising amongst members of professional groups, especially those who have taken the time to understand franchising.

One measure of the success of the franchising industry today is that we are seeing more and more businesses transitioning into a franchise model. I believe this is great for the industry and it's great for the economy. However, I do have to provide a caution here. Unfortunately, too many people want to franchise their company because they think it is a quick way to make money. A word of advice for those contemplating this move: Unless you have a good system in place, your documentation thoroughly prepared, and you invest up front, you will be heading for problems with the authorities and with franchisees. Simply starting a franchise and having the correct documentation is not sufficient for success. As a franchisor, you need to be able to provide to your franchisees ongoing support for—and innovation in—the brand, marketing, ongoing training, products, communications structures for sales reporting, IT and much more.

Franchising is not for everyone. If you want to join a franchise model but still do your own thing, then franchising is not for you. My recommendation to people who want to do their own thing, who want to be innovative and entrepreneurial, is to start your own business or look for something where you have more control. Franchising is all about following a system and protecting the brand. If you do join a franchise system, you only have the brand under licence; you don't actually own the brand, so you can't do what you like with it. It also costs a lot of money to buy, depending largely on the cost of the fit-out or the set-up.

I also have to say that often people enter into a franchise agreement the wrong way. They commit to the franchise without first doing their homework. They don't put all the right criteria in place before committing. For example, if they are going into partnership with their family, a friend or someone else, they often fail to document the details of how that partnership will work. Unless everything is thoroughly thought through before signing with a franchise, the partnership may later turn into a disaster. (See the Partnerships chapter for more information on this topic.)

Focus on the business first

So if you are keen to enter the franchising sector, be careful to do your research... and get your priorities right from the very beginning. John Maxwell, an internationally recognized business writer, tells the story of a farmer and his wife who one day bought a new property. Overnight they owned acres and acres of farmland and they could hardly wait to move from their present home to their new property. However, one night the two of them began to argue over what they were going to build first on the land. The wife desperately wanted to build the house first, but the farmer thought they should first build the barn. They bantered back and forth several times, until finally the farmer settled the argument by saying, "We are going to build the barn first, because the barn will build the house, the garage, the silo, the swing set and everything else."

The lesson in this story is that we must get our priorities right *before* launching into a new venture. I have found that some franchisees will open their store and then immediately begin to look around to buy their dream car and build extensions to their home. Much of their focus is taken away from the business during this critical start-up period. During the first couple of years of that franchise business opening, they invest their money and time on things external to the business. Then they wonder why their franchise business cannot sustain their repayments and why their lives are being pulled from one direction to another.

Franchising is no different to any other business model in that when you start your business, your primary focus must be on that business. Your priority should be to build the business first! Get your income and your business systems flowing before committing to other financial expenditures.

Another problem I have seen in franchising is that some new franchisees start off as poor people managers. They want to control every decision that involves the business. All they are doing is stifling their staff, when they should be growing them. Franchisees also need to learn to hire the right people, and then allow them to do their jobs. Franchisees need to focus on the key elements of the business and be willing to delegate. They need to learn to work *on* the business and not always *in* the business. Now, this depends on the size of the business, because there will always be an element of working *in* the business, but they do have to learn to be able to work *on* the business, which often means directing, training, motivating and setting the vision and goals for their employees.

I have also come to know franchisees who can't leave their business because they are what I would call 'control freaks'. They feel they can't leave the business because they don't trust their employees. Franchisees need to learn to trust their people enough to leave them to run the business for short periods of time.

A checklist to help you select the right franchise

So what do you look for when selecting the right franchise for you? Here is a checklist of what to look for (note that this is by no means an exhaustive list, but it provides a starting point for you):

1. *A proven system*. If the franchise has not been established for long, find out if they have invested in their systems and if they can demonstrate this investment. Ask them if it is a system that has been operating for some time. A franchise system includes the intellectual property, the supply chain (whether they order from the franchisor or direct from suppliers), and all the manuals (from running the business to marketing). That is the system that franchisees buy into.

2. *Ongoing support*. A good franchise system will offer ongoing support, not just training. In a franchise system, good ongoing support will include regular franchise meetings and an operational team who regularly visits franchise operations to offer advice on how to build the business and maintain quality standards. The team will also identify any additional training needs and then organise this through the training department. If it is a new franchise, find out what support systems and standards have been set in place. Find out what training and development there will be.

3. *Ongoing training.* Look for more than just the initial training. Ongoing training is vital to franchisees, as well as to your managers and staff. Depending on the franchise, this may include training in customer service. The operational team may earmark areas in which the franchisee needs additional training. For example, this may be in the area of cash flow, in which case a specific workshop will be run for the franchisee. It could also be in the area of customer service. Training is also included at the regular group franchisee meetings where the day session may be extended to two days and an outside guest is brought in to provide training in a specific area of the business, such as store merchandising.

Gloria Jean's Coffees works in partnership with William Angliss College in Victoria (Australia) to provide direct training to franchisee managers and their staff in the various stages of retail management (from Certificate I up to Certificate IV). This training builds their staff and their capabilities. This is in addition to the training that Gloria Jean's Coffees itself runs for staff, such as barista training, customer service and food standards.

4. *Buying power and product discounts.* As the franchise system grows, you should see benefits in buying power and in product supply. Buying power can lead to reduced fees in accounting services, insurances, telecommunications and even electricity. These cost reductions are often negotiated by the head office and this leads to immense savings in the cost of running a franchise operation. Note that these services can only be recommended by the franchisor because government legislation restricts the enforcement of third party purchases. The Australian Competition and Consumer Commission watches over this process. Being part of a franchise system provides additional benefits of lower prices and quality standards when it comes to the supply of products.

5. *Readily available finance.* Many of the banking systems today provide a franchising package. This, of course, will depend on the franchise system you are looking into. You will need to do a proper investigation of financial packages that will be available to you.

6. *Food Safety/Occupational Health and Safety.* All businesses need to be able to provide an Occupational Health and Safety system, but if the franchise you are looking at is a part of the food and beverage industry, then you will need to also understand food safety regulations.

7. *Value of the brand.* The value of the brand should continue to grow as each store opens, as each advertising message appears, as each product is sold, and as each service is provided. You will want to join a franchise whose brand value continues to grow.

8. *Group support.* In most franchises you have the opportunity to dialogue with other franchisees in the system. You should also take the opportunity to speak to a few existing franchisees in the system (if possible speak to more than one or two) before you make a decision to go forward. I am continually surprised at how many franchisees do not take up this opportunity. So many operate from a "This is my store" or an "I know everything" mentality. They are only concerned with their own situation and are not willing to learn from others who have more experience. In many cases, they think they know everything. In other cases, they are fearful to ask others for advice or they believe they are being an inconvenience to others. My advice is: This is going to be *your* business, so ask them!

Obstacles to watch out for

If you are looking to buy into a franchise system, here are some potential obstacles to look out for:

1. *A tired concept.* Watch out for franchise systems that have been around for some time and do not show evidence of ongoing innovation. Franchisors should always be looking at new ways to expand, grow and stay fresh. Avoid franchises that don't!

2. *Franchisors who provide limited or no support to the franchisee.* Be careful of franchisors who provide limited support to their franchisees. However, you need to keep in mind that some franchisees will believe that they are not getting adequate support from their franchisor, when in fact they are. Talk to quite

a few franchisees and you will soon get a true picture.

3. *Accountants and lawyers who can assist the franchisees to lift their results.* These days there are accountants and legal experts with extensive franchising expertise. As with any industry, it has taken many years for expertise to develop in the franchising sector. Unfortunately, there are many accountants and lawyers who still today provide very poor advice to franchisees. In fact, some are actually learning about franchising at the franchisee's expense. Accountants and bookkeepers who provide ongoing services to franchisees need to understand the franchise and retail sector. Accountants can easily charge high fees and process purchases and payments for franchisees without providing adequate advice and explanations of whether more money is going out than coming in. Many accountants also do not show how they are performing against set KPIs (Key Performance Indicators), especially where they have no experience in the retail and franchising sector. To help service providers like accountants and bookkeepers, a good franchisor will have in place recommended systems to measure sales, profit and loss, cost of goods, and so on.

4. *The potential to lose your nerve.* Everything may seem rose-coloured and exciting at the beginning, but there may come a time when you suddenly feel like you have made a mistake. At Gloria Jean's Coffees, we have had franchisees who have developed cold feet a week out from the store opening. In fact, even after they have opened the store, a few franchisees have walked around with a stunned look, their faces appearing like a deer caught in the car headlights. For many franchisees, everything may have seemed exciting during the interview process, the site selection and the training period, but suddenly reality kicks in. Some have actually worked in other franchisees' stores, loved the business and enjoyed the whole process, but once they get their own business, the fear factor starts to surface. So decide now whether you can handle this, and be prepared for this scenario!

5. *Don't expect the franchisor to run your business.* There are franchisees who have paid for a system believing that the franchisor will send someone in to run the business for them and tell them what to do. Franchisees need to understand that they

have invested in a system and a brand, and that they need to run with it themselves. They need to understand that they are now a leader to their staff and a leader in the local community. It is up to the franchisee to learn the business thoroughly and to seek help when help is needed. Understand that the franchisee needs to take responsibility for the success of the business.

Is franchising for you?

If you are interested in a franchise, you need to first ask yourself: "Is franchising for me?" To help you answer this question, here are three critical questions that may help you decide:

1. *What are your interests?* What are you passionate about? If you like working with animals, then there are franchises that may suit your interests, such as dog wash franchises. If you love helping people with their finances, then a financial lending franchise may suit you. If you don't like working outdoors, then don't look for a franchise that is outdoors, like tree-lopping and mowing lawns. If you don't like working with people and communicating with people, then there may not be too many options for you, but you certainly do not want to take on a food and beverage business or a service-orientated business.

2. *Are you willing to be committed 100% to a franchise business?* This is an important question because this business will dominate your thinking and govern your life. I know of a franchisee who opened a store and then said, "This is not what I thought it was!"
"Well, what did you have in mind?" I asked.

His response was that he thought he would have time to sit around drinking coffee and talking to customers all day. I say to franchisees who have this impression, "I have no idea where you got that opinion because it is nowhere in the presentations or in the early introductory meetings, and it is nowhere in the training program!" If you are serious about becoming a franchisee, then you need to realize that you are committed to looking after your staff, paying your bills, banking money, managing staff rosters, ordering products, cleaning the store, and so on.

3. *Are you financially capable of running your own business?*
You don't need to be an accountant, but you do need to start taking some interest in the difference between money coming in and money going out. You need to be able to manage your Key Performance Indicators. In the Gloria Jean's Coffees business your rent is fixed, and if a franchisee takes up the operating cost benefits that are available through insurance and other services, then you need to control your labour and your cost of goods. If these two get out of kilter, then it throws the whole profitability out for the business. Even if you have low rent and a high turnover, you can still be losing money. I am continually staggered at the number of franchisees across all franchise systems who have accountants or bookkeepers who do not understand retailing and who have no idea what they are doing! So you do need to know what you are doing, because it is *your* business.

4. *Are you able to follow a system?* In a franchising system, you will regularly be given instructions relating to new products, new guidelines and new systems. You can't just decide that you don't want to be part of a marketing program or you don't want to introduce a new product that is part of the overall system. To be successful in franchising, you will need to follow a system that has been tried and tested. In fact, the system is the very reason why people buy into a franchise.

take action |
NOW!

one: If you find that you don't enjoy your work, consider getting into franchising—it gives so many people a wonderful opportunity to have fun while earning a living.

two: If, after reading everything I have said so far in this chapter, you are still interested in giving franchising a go, then here are a few last tips:

• Do your research so that you understand what franchising is all about. Educate yourself so that you understand what your role will be, what your rights will be, and what your responsibility will be as part of any particular franchise community. Take a look at the Franchise Council of Australia website: www.franchise.org.au. There are also many worthwhile articles in *Franchising Magazine,* which is available in many newsagencies.

• Search out accounting firms, legal firms and franchising consultants who have in-depth franchising expertise.

• Make sure you get an opportunity to do your own due diligence and thoroughly work through all your questions before proceeding with them. Whilst risk can never be totally eliminated, this will help to minimize any inherent risks.

To be continued...

"If at first you don't succeed, sky diving is not for you!"
Spotted on a car bumper sticker

I love this quote and often use it in my presentations to business groups. The topic of this book is quite serious, but we need to stop and laugh at ourselves every so often. We need to laugh at life and laugh with those around us. We only get one life, so make the most of it. Live it to the full!

The title of this last chapter is 'To Be Continued...' This means your life doesn't stop the day you reach a major milestone. Your life doesn't stop the day you get married, the day you start a job or the day you retire. Whatever levels of success you have already reached and no matter your achievements so far, you are still here on this earth to continue to succeed in your endeavours.

Today is the first day of the rest of your life. Today is a new day in your relationships and in your business. Today you are perched on the edge of your destiny. What are you going to do with it? In the Book of Esther in the Old Testament, young Queen Esther was in the right place at the right time in the history of her people. As a beauty queen entrant, she faced an important and dangerous challenge. God had chosen Esther to intercede on behalf of her people. And she was willing to rise to the challenge; she was even willing to sacrifice her life for the sake of her people. She took the challenge, made the right decision, and her action literally saved her nation. She was born for such a time as this. You too have been born for such a day as this: today!

What is the challenge before you? What is it that is hindering your success? Are you still fiddling around, making excuses? Or do you feel you are not ready? Perhaps you need to be reminded that standing still does not get you closer to your destiny. Standing still means you will never arrive at the resources you need to fulfill your vision and your destiny.

I recently read the following statement from *The Word for Today* daily devotional:

Everybody wants to be thin, but nobody wants to diet.

Everybody wants more money, but nobody wants more work.

Successful people form the habit of doing things unsuccessful people don't like to do.

The bookends of success are – commitment and consistency. Without commitment you'll never start. Without consistency, you'll never finish.

Getting started is the hard part. That's because we have so many reasons not to start. So, here are some helpful suggestions:

1. *Start with yourself.* Don't wait for others to start for you or fall in line behind your plans. If you want those around you to respond differently, give them a different set of attitudes and actions to respond to. Acknowledge that *you* are responsible.

2. *Start early.* There's an old saying that Noah didn't wait for his ship to come in—he built one himself. Hard work is just an accumulation of the easy things you didn't do when you should have. The truth is that the work doesn't seem quite so hard when you stop putting it off.

3. *Start small.* Just take the first step. You can't do Step 2 until you've done Step 1. Taking the first step to prioritise your life focuses you in the right direction. And don't expect to understand all that's required at this early stage.

4. *Start now.* What are you waiting for? Until you finish school? Get married? Have kids? Your kids leave home? You retire? You die? If you wait long enough, you'll have only one regret—that

you didn't start now.

Many people die with dreams still inside them. What a tragedy. Don't let that be you!

In the Book of Romans in the New Testament, the apostle Paul stated, "Don't become so well adjusted to your culture that you fit into it without ever thinking." (Romans 12:2) Don't be a thermometer, be a thermostat. Thermometers simply *reflect* the temperature around them, whereas thermostats *set* the temperature. Better still, thermostats actually *lift* the temperature. Most of us are like thermometers reflecting the culture around us. We buy things others buy, say things others say, wear things others wear, and value things others value. There might be some slight variations, but sadly most of the time we don't set the climate for the world we live in; we simply adjust to it.

Learn to take life to the next level. Upgrade your life to another level. This means that you will need to actually change the environment in which you've been placed. You can set the trends, raise the values and establish the pace. Become a pacesetter. Become an influencer rather than allow others to influence you. Do it well and others will follow.

Learn to focus on the solutions, not the problems. When we focus on the problems and issues that come up, we neglect to look at the solutions and we never resolve the problems. Problems won't go away in your business and in your relationships until you face them with solutions.

If you are solutions-oriented, then you are half-way to being vision-oriented. Pastor David Yonggi Cho is pastor of Yoido Full Gospel Church in South Korea, the largest church in the world. He once stated, "Show me your vision and I'll show you your future." If you have no vision, you have no future. If you would like a future marked with success, then grab a hold of your vision now. Write it down and share it around.

So do you believe your life is *to be continued?* Do you believe your business has a future and *is to be continued?* Do you believe your relationships have a future and are *to be continued?* Or do you see the final chapter of your life as 'The End'… with no future?

If this chapter is challenging you, then you may need to refresh your vision, reset your sails, and set your course towards your great future. Develop the passion and the commitment to move ahead and don't allow anyone else to drag you off that course. No matter what age you are right now and no matter what stage you are at in life, you've still got your whole life stretched out ahead of you. The lessons from this book are actually quite simple. I want to encourage you to adopt these lessons to enhance your business, your relationships and your life. Use this book to catapult yourself closer towards achieving your vision.

Support for Great Community Causes

There are many charities, causes and ministries that you can support. In business and in life, you need to learn to be generous and to live beyond yourself. Here are some great causes with which to align yourself personally or through your company, whether through sponsorship, donations or by simply contributing resources and services. Your involvement with a great cause will bring tremendous benefit to your company, your staff, your customers and, at the same time, those in need—the direct beneficiaries of the cause.

Mercy Ministries—a residential program for young women in crisis. Mercy Ministries is a non profit organisation dedicated to providing homes and care for young women suffering the effects of eating disorders, self harm, abuse, depression, unplanned pregnancies and other life-controlling issues.

Mercy Ministries Australia
Phone: +612 9659 4180
Web: www.mercyministries.com.au

Mercy Ministries NZ
Phone: +64 9 308 6778
Web: www.mercyministries.org.nz

Mercy Ministries UK
Phone: +44 (0) 1535 642 042
Web: www.mercyministries.co.uk

Mercy Ministries US
Phone: (615)-831-6987
Web: www.mercyministries.org

Teen Challenge—Teen Challenge provides practical solutions to people with life-controlling problems—primarily drugs and alcohol. The program aims to eliminate their self destructive habits by meeting the needs of the whole person... not only dealing with the addiction, but also rebuilding their self-image, work ethic, spiritual awareness and relationships.

Teen Challenge New South Wales
Phone: 1800 679 657
Web: www.one80tc.org

Teen Challenge Queensland
Phone: (07) 3422 1500
Web: www.teenchallenge.org.au

Teen Challenge South Australia
Phone: (08) 8431 9566
Web: www.tc.asn.au

Teen Challenge Western Australia
Phone: (08) 9309 5255
Web: www.teenchallengewa.org.au

Teen Challenge Victoria
Phone: (03) 5852 3777
Web: www.teenchallenge.com.au

Teen Challenge Centralia (Northern Territory)
Phone: 0411 625 467

Teen Challenge International
Web: www.globaltc.org

Compassion—a child sponsorship program. Compassion International exists as a Christian child advocacy ministry that releases children from spiritual, physical, economic and social poverty and enables them to become responsible, fulfilled Christian adults.

Compassion Australia
Phone: 1800 224 453
Web: www.compassion.com.au

Compassion International
Phone: (800) 336-7676 (USA)
Web: www.compassion.com

Compassion UK
Phone: 01932 836490
Web: www.compassionuk.org

Opportunity International — a global leader of microfinance and enterprise development. Opportunity International is where you can fund a Trust Bank that creates jobs in third world countries. A Trust Bank can continue to provide ongoing jobs and equipment for people to start businesses. These people then pay back their small interest loan, which is again loaned out so other people can start a new business.

Opportunity International Australia
Phone: (02) 9270 3300
Web: www.opportunity.org.au

Opportunity International USA
Phone: (toll-free) 800.7WE.WILL (793-9455)
Web: www.opportunity.org

The Gloria Jean's Coffees' experience

Gloria Jean's Coffees' experience proves the benefits of community support. Staff get behind the company's commitment to causes by raising funds themselves and providing word-of-mouth support. Customers also come into Gloria Jean's Coffees stores and say they've heard about the company's community work. They also visually see the company's commitment through the Mercy Ministries money boxes and promotional leaflets on store counters, as well as the company's other promotional activities on display throughout the store. Evidence shows that customers believe this is fantastic and that they are keen to support a company that's willing to sow back into the community.

Acknowledgements

When you start your journey in life, in business and in relationships, there are many people who play a key part. There's no way that every person is able to be mentioned in this situation, but there are certainly individuals who have come across my path and who assisted me or challenged me to the next stage of my journey. I'd like to mention a few of those people here.

In my advertising days—especially in the early years, but even as I moved a few years into the business—one of our key Group Account Directors had a real impact on me. John Bradstock went on to become Managing Director and then became a worldwide influence in DDB Needham Advertising Worldwide. John showed confidence in me even though I was young, immature and had almost no experience in business. Through his encouragement and support I was able to grow and realise my potential.

During my days with DDB Needham Advertising, we launched McDonald's into Australia and saw McDonald's go through tough times and build a business through commitment, marketing and franchising. There are actually many people I was involved with during this time and who I could thank, but I would like to name three people who kept the business simple and kept people focussed. I learned an enormous amount from watching them in action. One of those was Peter Ritchie, who was with McDonald's in the early days. Another was Bob Mansfield, who came on the scene a bit later, but was part of the catalyst for the growth of McDonald's. And then there's Charlie Bell. These guys were able to keep things simple and keep everyone focussed, and that gave me enormous challenge in relation to the agency and through starting a new business.

Then in 1993, when I was 47 years of age, my wife and I moved our church base and started attending Hills Christian Life Centre (now Hillsong Church). We saw the vision that Pastors Brian and Bobbie Houston had—a vision which embraced more than just the local scene. It encompassed Australia and the world, even in those early years. We have been privileged to see that vision become a reality and to see the church take on the challenge of helping people in the community. This inspired us to realise there was more to life than just 'getting by' and 'paying the bills'.

In fact, when the opportunity came to purchase the worldwide rights for Gloria Jean's Coffees, the Hillsong vision was one of the things that inspired us. If a church based in a small part of Sydney could not only become influential Australia-wide, but actually become recognised and inspirational throughout the world (especially through music), then who said a business in Australia could not achieve the same thing!

In 1995 Nabi and Angela Saleh approached Sue and me about the opportunity that had come across their path to take on Gloria Jean's Coffees in Australia. Nabi and I visited the US and looked at the model and decided to negotiate the rights for a ten-year period plus a ten-year renewal option. I want to thank them for the opportunity for us to become co-founders in Australia and establish a phenomenal and exciting brand. Then to be able to take on the world with such a brand… It has been an exciting ride for both of us!

The most important human beings in my life are my wife, Sue, and my family, and I thank them for their support and their encouragement—especially when I started to get discouraged both through my years in advertising and with Gloria Jean's Coffees. During these times they helped me to be able to get my focus back. All of which enables me to be at a point today where I can share in this book some of the lessons I have learned.

I also want to thank two key people who helped me get this book out. First, my daughter-in-law, Meg, who pulled everything together for me and coordinated all the logistics. Then there was Mark Badham, who helped me put into words the messages I present at my speaking engagements.

Of course, the one to thank above all else is my God who gives me the vision and the dreams, and who has a destiny and a future for my life. When we realise that life isn't about religion, that we can have a personal relationship with God for ourselves, we move into a whole new, exciting and miraculous journey in every area of life—in our relationships, in our businesses, and in our social life.

Recommended Books

Here is a list of books I would highly recommend you read and from which I have quoted in this book.

The Bible. Scripture I have quoted was taken from a variety of translations. However, I have mostly quoted from the New King James Version. Copyright.© 1982 by Thomas Nelson, inc. Used by permission. All rights reserved.

Keith Abraham, *Inspirational Insights* (Australia: Passion Press, 2006).

Jim Collins, *Good to Great* (New York: Random House Business Books, 2001).

Thomas L Friedman, *The World is Flat: A Brief History of the Twenty-first Century* (New York: Farrar, Straus and Giroux, 2006).

Bob and Debby Gass, *The Word for Today* (UCB Australia: Brisbane).

The Word for Today is a daily devotional that has constant challenges and leadership principles for business people today. Although the first copy is free, my recommendation is to provide a donation to UCB so that you receive the quarterly books as they are published. A free introductory copy of this daily devotional may be obtained from UCB Australia (free for Australian residents only) or from UCB United Kingdom (free for UK residents only). Australia freecall: 1800 007 770. Web: www.ucb.co.uk and www.ucb.com.au.

Malcolm Gladwell, *The Tipping Point* (London: Abacus, 2001).

Seth Godin, *Purple Cow* (New York: Portfolio, 2003).

David Jenkins, *What Great Retailers Do* (Melbourne: Baraka House Publishing, 2006).

Max Lucado, *Cure for the Common Life* (Nashville: Thomas Nelson, 2006).

John Maxwell, *The Maxwell Leadership Bible* (Nashville: Thomas Nelson, 2002).

Jerry Savelle, *Free To Be Yourself* (Texas: Jerry Savelle Ministries, 2006).

Author's note: Every effort has been made to identify copyright holders of extracts in this book. The publishers would be pleased to hear from any copyright holders who have not been acknowledged.

About the Author

Peter Irvine is a successful businessman, author and motivational speaker. He is increasingly in demand as a speaker to audiences across the globe on many business topics, including marketing, franchising, vision and sponsorship.

He has achieved remarkable success in helping to launch two of the most recognized brands in Australia: Gloria Jean's Coffees and McDonald's. During his advertising career, he helped to build the McDonald's brand in Australia.

Peter has worked in the advertising industry in Australia for over 30 years. During most of that time he worked for DDB Needham Advertising in Sydney, eventually becoming Managing Director.

As co-founder of Gloria Jean's Coffees, Peter has been instrumental in establishing one of Australia's fastest-growing franchises. He and his business partner, Nabi Saleh, launched Gloria Jean's Coffees in Australia in 1996, and 10 years later they purchased the international brand name. They now have over 750 stores across 30 countries. Today over 85% of Australians recognise the Gloria Jean's Coffees name and associate it with specialty coffee.

When Gloria Jean's Coffees began in Australia, experts in the coffee and franchising industries warned Peter he would fail, that Australians would not embrace flavoured or take-away coffee. Today Gloria Jean's Coffees has succeeded beyond all expectations. And it has done so by destroying mindsets and setting trends in the industry. For instance, Gloria Jean's Coffees introduced frequent sipper cards and chai tea latte to the Australian café industry. Gloria Jean's Coffees also pioneered the widespread adoption of takeaway hot drinks and a pay-before-you-drink culture. Ultimately, the company has changed the way Australians drink coffee.

These days Peter Irvine spends much of his time sharing the secrets to his success. He speaks at conventions, seminars, forums, churches, small business functions and community functions. He is passionate about helping business people grow their businesses and their personal lives. As a Christian, he is also a strong proponent of working and living for a cause beyond ourselves… by supporting churches, charities and causes.

Peter is involved in consulting to companies that either want to explore franchising, are already franchised and yet keen to grow to another level, or that want to take their franchise overseas. Companies also utilize Peter Irvine's services to explore opportunities to get involved in charities or community sponsorships and how best to approach these types of relationships.

Peter and his wife, Sue, are long-time, committed members of a local church in Sydney. They live in the north-western suburbs of Sydney. They have two sons and four grandchildren.

Contact Details

PR Irvine Pty Ltd
Email: peter@prirvine.com
Website: www.prirvine.com

PO Box 14
Round Corner
New South Wales 2158
Australia

Peter Irvine's Services

Resources: You can buy additional copies of this book online. You may also wish to add your name and contact details to Peter Irvine's mailing list for future release of other books and helpful resources.

Speaking: Peter Irvine is available to speak at conventions, seminars, forums, small business functions and community functions.

Franchising: He is also involved in consulting to companies that either want to explore franchising, are already franchised and yet keen to grow to another level, or that want to take their franchise overseas.

Charities and community sponsorships: Companies also utilize Peter Irvine's services to explore opportunities to get involved in charities or community sponsorships and how best to approach these types of relationships.

Achievers Group: Peter is also part of the Achievers Group team. Our slogan is: Achieving through People, Strategies and Systems. Join the Achievers Group mailing list for your fortnightly vitamin intake:
Web Registration: www.achieversgroup.com.au/registration_form.html

Email: tony@achieversgroup.com.au

Achievers Group Pty Ltd
Level 1, 284 Bobbin Head Road, North Turramurra, NSW 2074, Australia
Phone: +61 - 2 9440 7373
Web: www.achieversgroup.com.au